From the Inside Out

The Power of Reflection and Self-Awareness

Paula Jorde Bloom

NEW HORIZONS

EDUCATIONAL CONSULTANTS AND LEARNING RESOURCES

LAKE FOREST, ILLINOIS 60045-0863

Library of Congress Cataloging-in-Publication Data

Bloom, Paula J.
    From the inside out : the power of reflection and
self-awareness / Paula Jorde Bloom.
        p. cm. — (Director's toolbox)
    Includes bibliographical references.
    ISBN-13: 978-0-9621894-9-4
    ISBN-10: 0-9621894-9-9

    1. Early childhood education--United States--
Administration. 2. Early childhood education--
Vocational guidance--United States. I. Title.
II. Series.

LB2822.6.B55 2007   372.12
                        QBI07-600114

New Horizons Learning Resources, Inc.
616 Smith Ave.
Lake Bluff, IL 60044
Newhorizons4@comcast.net
847.295.8131
www.newhorizonsbooks.net

Books in **The Director's Toolbox Management Series** are available at quantity discounts for use in training programs. For information on bulk quantity rates or how to purchase a **Trainer's Guide** for this book, contact the publisher.

Illustrations – *Marc Bermann*

Design – *Stan Burkat*

CONTENTS

Chapter

About the Author

Paula Jorde Bloom holds a joint appointment as Michael W. Louis Endowed Chair of the McCormick Center for Early Childhood Leadership and professor of early childhood education at National Louis University in Wheeling, Illinois. As one of the country's leading experts on early childhood leadership and program management issues, Dr. Bloom is a frequent keynote speaker at state, national, and international conferences and consultant to professional organizations and state agencies.

Paula received her master's and doctoral degrees from Stanford University. She has taught preschool and kindergarten, designed and directed a child care center, and served as administrator of a campus laboratory school. She is the author of numerous journal articles and several widely read books, including *Avoiding Burnout, A Great Place to Work, Blueprint for Action, Circle of Influence, Workshop Essentials,* and *Leadership in Action.* She is co-author with Teri Talan of the *Program Administration Scale.*

Acknowledgements

Writing this book was truly an inside-out experience for me. I am turning 60 this year and approaching this important decade marker seemed like a good time to step back and reflect on my own personal and professional journey. As coincidence would have it, just as I started writing I was diagnosed with cancer...again. Being struck by lighting twice has an interesting way of putting one's priorities into sharp focus.

I am indebted to those scholars, educators, and spiritual leaders whose writings have inspired me to reach deeper and ask hard questions of myself—among others, Parker Palmer, Wayne Muller, Dave Ellis, Richard Carlson, Frederic Hudson, Margie Carter, Tom Dickelman, Harold Kushner, Bonnie and Roger Neugebauer, and Margaret Wheatley. I hope that I have passed on a small measure of what I have learned in the process. My thanks to Heather Knapp and Lisa Boggess for help in tracking down resources for this book. In fine-tuning the manuscript I am deeply appreciative of the helpful feedback I received from Jill Bella, Teri Talan, Ann Hentschel, and Catherine Cauman.

WHOOOOOO ARE YOU?

CHAPTER 1

Becoming a Self-Mentor

Socrates summed up the secret to a meaningful life in two simple words—"Know thyself." Self-awareness means knowing your needs and values, your strengths and limitations, your passions, and your idiosyncratic quirks. It means having a deep appreciation of what makes you a unique specimen on this planet. On a deeper level, self-awareness means knowing how you react in different situations and accepting full responsibility for your feelings and actions.

Having a better understanding of oneself is the first step to having a better relationship with others. This is because self-awareness provides a window to expand our understanding about other points of view and perspectives. While the importance of self-awareness is readily understood by most people, achieving it is easier said than done. Even Benjamin Franklin acknowledged this when he wrote in his *Poor Richard's Almanac* that "There are three things extremely hard: steel, diamonds, and to know one's self."

The reason self-awareness is so difficult to achieve is that it involves an ongoing assessment of our assumptions, beliefs, and values, and the mental models that shape our behavior and guide our actions both at work and in our personal lives. The goal of this kind of reflection is not merely to see who we are and better understand ourselves today, but to envision what we might become tomorrow. It is a lifelong process—a journey of self-discovery, meaning making, and identity shaping.

Why Self-Awareness Is So Important

The importance of self-awareness is based on George Kelly's construct theory, first published in 1955, and his notion that every person is a psychologist. Kelly believed that people's common sense ideas and their own theories about life and relationships are enormously rich sources of knowledge about human affairs. The central thesis of his approach is that we do not merely react to events; we are in charge of what we do in the world and have the potential to recreate ourselves.

Two other social psychologists have been influential in promoting the self-awareness movement of personal psychology. In his 1987 book *Beginning with Ourselves*, David Hunt calls the approach *inside-out psychology*. He contrasts this to an outside-in approach which leaves human affairs to the experts. The same year, Donald Schön published his seminal work *Educating the Reflective Practitioner*. This book, as well, gave credence to the idea that achieving professional competence is a dynamic process involving continual inquiry and renewal.

Throughout the course of life, individuals have a compelling need to make sense out of their experiences and choices. In Robert Kegan's words, "The activity of being a person is an activity of meaning making." Self-awareness is central to meaning making. Lives cannot be understood without an appreciation of the context in which they are lived. Self-awareness helps one connect broad concepts to their situation-specific relevance.

Being self-aware is at the core of what Howard Gardner refers to as *intrapersonal intelligence* or what Daniel Goleman refers to as *emotional intelligence*. Self-awareness is the capacity to be introspective and examine thoughts and feelings. It means being aware of both our mood and our thoughts about that mood. Self-awareness includes:

- affective awareness—the knowledge of one's feelings, attitudes, moods, and outlook

- ethical awareness—the ability to set one's principles and moral priorities

- self-regulation—the ability to monitor one's thoughts, actions, and behavior

- metacognition—the ability to be aware of one's thought processes

Self-awareness, in short, means the ability to identify and name our emotional states. The ability to understand the link between our emotions, our thoughts, and our actions is necessary before we can manage our emotional states. When people can recognize and manage their own emotions, they are better equipped to understand the emotions of others. Self-aware people are attuned to their emotional reflexes. This means they are better able to modify their actions and behavior in different situations. The good news is that just being aware of the importance of being aware increases self-awareness.

Self-awareness also means having a clear picture of our internal motives—those things that drive us to say what we say and do what we do. Peeling away the layers of our motivations is not always a comfortable process, but it is a necessary step if our goal is to become an authentic leader known for personal integrity. Central to this process is gaining clarity about what we perceive our purpose in life to be and how we define success.

Becoming a Reflective Practitioner

The capacity to reflect and engage in candid introspection is at the core of achieving self-awareness. Reflective practitioners have the ability to think both creatively and self-critically about what they are doing. Individuals who use a variety of reflective approaches have a better awareness of their strengths and weaknesses and can better understand, monitor, and adjust their behavior in personal and professional interactions.

Joseph Saban and his associates have identified three different types of reflection. The most common they refer to as *reflection-on-action*. This is simply a replay of an experience in order to review, revisit, or recall what happened, like replaying a videotape. *Reflection-in-action* refers to a kind of out-of-body experience in which we watch ourselves act and simultaneously reflect about the decisions we are making. A third type of reflection is referred to as *reflection-for-action*. This is a predictive process for forecasting how we will use what we have learned from reflection-in-action and reflection-on-action. It involves consciously adjusting our behaviors based on our reflections.

The content or substance of reflection goes through a change as individuals gain mastery in their profession. They are better able to recognize the gap between their *espoused theories* (what they say) and their *theories-in-action* (what they actually do). The formula for bridging this *knowing-doing gap* is pretty straight forward and consists of several questions:

- What do I do?

- Why do I do what I do?

- Is what I do achieving the results I want?

- How might I do things differently?

These are not rhetorical questions; they are intended to raise consciousness, to challenge complacency, and to engender a higher order of professional practice.

Using Assessments to Build Self-Awareness

As humans we have an insatiable appetite for understanding what makes us tick—how we think, how we process information, how we make decisions, how we learn, what makes us feel good, and what makes us feel miserable. There is certainly no shortage of formal and informal self-assessment tools to help build self-awareness. Some tools offer quick snapshots—a questionnaire that can be completed in ten minutes and scored independently. Others are quite lengthy and must be administered by a certified psychologist or trainer.

It's hard to see the picture when you are in the frame.

Michael Brandwein

At the risk of oversimplifying, self-assessment instruments can be divided into two broad categories of awareness building: *prescriptive and descriptive*. Prescriptive assessments compare a person's traits to those of a model teacher or administrator and diagnose the individual's strengths and weaknesses in relation to that ideal. Descriptive instruments, on the other hand, are the ones that say, "This is your type, your style, your preference. It is no better or worse than any other, just different." Descriptive instruments aim to raise self-awareness and give insights into the differences among individuals. These instruments often result in "Ah-ha!" moments, opening the door to changes in behavior.

The goal of self-assessment is to improve professional practice and job fulfillment. When we use the term *professional practice*, we're really talking about *competence* in whatever role the early childhood educator holds. Engaging in self-assessment then should give practitioners greater awareness of their strengths as well the areas of as knowledge and skill that need to be improved. Using William Howell's levels of competence, we can think of this as moving to progressively higher stages in learning—from *unconscious incompetence* ("I don't even know what I don't know") to *conscious incompetence* ("Omigosh, I have so much to learn") to *conscious competence* ("I am keenly aware of what I know and how it impacts my performance") to *unconscious competence* ("I am on automatic pilot").

From Reflection and Self-Awareness to Self-Mentoring

It is one thing to be self-aware, to acquire information from reflection and formal and informal self-assessment, and quite another to apply that information to concrete behavioral changes. No doubt about it, the most effective professionals hold a transformational view of human growth and change. They see themselves as active agents in describing, interpreting, and shaping their behavior. In other words, they are self-mentors.

The great Roman philosopher Cicero is credited with saying, "No one can give you better advice than yourself." That is really the premise of self-mentoring. Self-mentoring is essentially self-directed learning. It means intentionally developing and strengthening those aspects of who you are that will move you toward who you want to be. Self-mentoring requires that you not only get an accurate picture of your real self—who you are now—but also a strong image of your ideal self—the person you aspire to become.

One vital aspect of self-development, stresses Richard Boyatzis, a leader in the self-directed learning movement, is striking a balance between what it is about ourselves we want to preserve and what we want to change. His research shows that people who successfully change in sustainable ways cycle through the following stages:

- First, they create an image of their *ideal* self. They ask themselves the question, "Who do I want to be?"

- Second, they come to terms with their *real* self. They ask themselves, "Who am I?" "What are my strengths—where do my ideal and my real self overlap? What are my gaps—where do my ideal and real differ?"

- Third, they are deliberate in crafting a learning agenda. They ask themselves, "How can I build on my strengths while reducing my gaps?"

- Fourth, they experiment with and practice new behaviors, thoughts, and feelings to the point of mastery. They ask themselves, "What subtle adjustments can I make to refine and expand my repertoire of skills and abilities?"

- Finally, they develop trusting relationships that help, support, and encourage each step in process. They ask themselves, "Who can I count on to give me direct and candid feedback and keep me on track?"

In sum, the goal of self-mentoring is to create the internal dialogue that will help you shape your future in deliberate and conscious ways.

Getting Started

Sadly, many people wait for a crisis before beginning to think deeply about themselves. The job of becoming a self-mentor is really about developing the disposition of lifelong learning and self-transformation. Ongoing self-reflection is central to that process. This means becoming fully aware of what you really want in all areas of your life and being able to invent new possibilities that enable you to unleash your passions. Here are some questions to get you started.

- What's really important to you? What do you value most?

- What special talents make you unique?

- What qualities do you most admire in others?

- How do you define personal success? When have you felt most successful?

- How have you used your knowledge, skill, and special talents to make a difference in the world?

- When have you felt most alive, energized, and excited about work? When have you felt most depleted and discouraged about work?

- Is there something you've always longed to do but never quite had the courage to do?

Knowing others is intelligence; knowing yourself is true wisdom. Mastering others is strength; mastering yourself is true power.

Tao Te Ching

- How do you handle adversity? Are you quick to blame others when things don't go well, or do you take ownership for the outcome of your decisions and actions?

- When do you feel most at peace?

- Have you achieved a reasonable sense of balance in your life between your personal and professional pursuits?

- Do you know how to regulate your emotions, or do your emotions get in the way in your interpersonal relationships?

- If you had unlimited time and resources, what would you choose to do?

- Do you often compare yourself to others?

- What do you want more of in your relationships? What do you want less of?

- How would you describe your favorite coworker? How would you describe your least favorite coworker? How are these individuals different? How are they like or not like you?

- What legacy do you want to pass on?

The Power of Journaling

Keeping a journal is a great way to promote self-awareness. Your journal doesn't need to be fancy; a plain memo pad or notebook will do. The key is the process—a candid dialogue with yourself, sharing thoughts, reflections, insights, frustrations, and joys about memorable moments in your life. Your journal can be a detailed record of your experiences or your perceptions and observations about critical incidents and interactions that have occurred. It can serve as a way to vent your emotions, analyze your actions, or capture in writing your hopes and dreams for the future.

Self-mentoring means cultivating your own professional growth through reflection, networking, and seeking out appropriate resources. The process clearly requires motivation and self-discipline. *From the Inside Out* is designed as a guide to support you in that process. In the following chapters you'll have an opportunity to reflect on where you are in your journey through adulthood—the joys and challenges you've experienced, as well as your hopes and dreams for the decades ahead.

- You'll be presented with thought-provoking questions to help you be more aware of your beliefs and attitudes and examine how your core values shape your self-perception and influence your decision making;

- You'll gain insights as you complete a variety of self-assessments that will help you better understand your temperament, your communication strengths and pitfalls, and your preferred learning style;

- You'll have an opportunity to gauge the gap between your current and your ideal work environment and determine the factors that impact your job satisfaction; and

- You'll become the architect of your own future by engaging in a number of exercises to help you explore new possibilities and articulate a compelling and achievable vision.

From the Inside Out is not a book about formulas. It is a book about the reflective process necessary to achieve the personal and professional identity to which you aspire. It is a book designed to promote self-discovery and introduce ways to stretch your potential and connect your daily actions to a deeper sense of purpose. It is a book that will help you take charge of your life *from the inside out.*

The most practical thing we can achieve in any kind of work is insight into what is happening inside us as we do it. The more familiar we are with our inner terrain, the more surefooted our teaching—and living—becomes.

Parker Palmer

CHAPTER 2

Navigating the Adult Years

"I wish that I knew what I know now, when I was younger." You don't need to be a superstar like Rod Stewart to understand the significance of the lyrics in his hit single, "Ooh La La." All of us have looked back on events in years past with a sense of profound amazement at our naïveté and narrow perspective. Age and experience do bring insight, however painful those lessons are sometimes. While we all take for granted that we change with age in our physical capacities and our judgment and perspective, few of us are really conscious of the subtle shifts in point of view as they are happening.

Making career choices, negotiating relationships and commitments, balancing personal and professional obligations, and navigating the ups and downs of life transitions is what adulthood is about. Self-awareness is essential to understanding the significance of life events and integrating lessons learned from the challenges we have faced. Drawing on developmental age and stage theories, this chapter looks at the overarching themes of adulthood as they relate to motivation, life choices, and personal and professional effectiveness.

All Adults Have Basic Needs

As humans we all have primal feelings and needs. Some needs are biological and relate to our survival—the need for food, sleep, air, water, sex, and the avoidance of pain. Others are psychological—these are the visceral forces that motivate us to make decisions and take actions. Most often these secondary needs are at an unconscious level. Once recognized, though, they help explain our individual stories. Based on the seminal work of Henry Murray, psychologists have identified four primary needs that help explain our internal motivation systems.

The need for affiliation. We are by nature social beings. We want to be accepted by others and achieve harmonious relationships. Although we may enjoy some solitude and time alone, we all need family, friends, and colleagues who are caring, supportive, and appreciative. This is because our sense of identity is largely shaped by our social interactions. Being a member of a group—belonging—nurtures our self-image, confirming that others value us.

We know from research that people engaged in mutually supportive relationships cope better with the stress inherent in their personal and professional lives. By working with others who care and share, we gain an increased understanding of ourselves and develop more realistic coping strategies to deal with the stressors that confront us.

The need for achievement. Anyone spending time with infants and toddlers can't help but be in awe at their internal drive to master their environment—to lift their heads, roll over, grasp and pull, communicate with their caregivers, and master the crawling, cruising, climbing, and walking milestones of physical development. Preschoolers exhibit the same kind of persistence in learning to ride a bicycle, climb to the top of the playground structure, or write their names.

Our need to master our world doesn't end in childhood. Throughout our lives, we negotiate new challenges, achieve goals, and feel successful. While everyone yearns to feel needed, challenged, and recognized for work well done, individuals differ in their drive for achievement. A person high in achievement motivation will choose more difficult tasks and persist longer in overcoming obstacles than a person low in achievement motivation.

The need for power and to feel significant. Although it has negative connotations, power is a dynamic that exists in virtually all adult/child and adult/adult relationships. Our need for power fuels our desire to have influence on others, to achieve recognition and prestige, and to control the behavior of others, good or bad.

All humans want to know that they matter in the world. The need to feel significant is what drives people to place enormous value on status symbols like job titles, designer labels, and expensive cars. The desire to feel important is what causes people to beam with pride when they are photographed with a celebrity or go to extraordinary lengths to get into the *Guinness Book of Records*. It is also why we get so annoyed when the clerk at a department store ignores us or when the doctor keeps us waiting beyond our scheduled appointment.

In our work environments, our need for influence fuels our desire to be involved in the decisions that directly impact us. Research in industry and other sectors of the economy confirms my own findings in early childhood work settings—employees' perceptions of being valued, respected, and involved in decision making is a more potent predictor of job satisfaction than level of salary or benefits.

The need for intimacy. While our need for affiliation focuses on social relationships, our need for intimacy focuses on one-to-one interactions—our desire for warm, loving, and caring attachments. All you need to do is look at the instant success of online match-making sites like eHarmony and Match.com to understand the strength of this human drive. Linked to survival of the species, the need for intimacy promotes coupling, nesting, and creating the close bonds that ensure our well-being over the long haul.

In his book *Social Intelligence*, Daniel Goleman provides compelling evidence of the physical and psychological benefits of strong and stable intimate relationships. Goleman states that loneliness has little to do with how much time people actually spend by themselves or how many social contacts they have. What matters, he emphasizes, is the quality of our interactions. It is the paucity of intimate contacts that leads to loneliness. Our need for warmth and supportiveness, for bonds that permit self-disclosure, is directly related to our well-being. The lonelier people feel, the more compromised their immune and cardiovascular systems. In nourishing relationships, partners help each other manage their distressing feelings and put things in perspective.

So how does understanding our basic motivations and needs support our personal and professional growth as early childhood educators? A major assumption of motivation theory is that our behavior is driven by an internal state of disequilibrium. In other words, when we lack something, we are driven to correct the imbalance. Reflecting on the link between our motivations and our behavior can help us see the way in which our actions may be prompted by a perceived void in one or more of the four areas of basic need. Such self-awareness can help us become more sensitive in our personal and professional interactions.

The Impact of the Early Years on Adulthood

As an early childhood educator, you already understand the importance of your work in shaping the foundations for children's healthy development. While they may debate the precise ages, most child psychologists and educators agree that the preschool years are crucial for laying the foundation for a person's self-identity and that the core elements of self-esteem are well solidified by age 14. In other words, the earliest experiences in our lives provide an anchor for our adult reality.

Reflecting back on your own childhood can both strengthen your understanding of the vital work you do and provide insight into why you think and behave the way you do as an adult. Such reflection also often provides insight into your motivations for entering the field of early childhood.

Think of the key messages you heard from your parents, grandparents, siblings, teachers, and other significant figures in your life about what you could do or what you could accomplish in life. These are often the same messages we say when we talk to ourselves. "I'm really good at ..." or "I'll never be able to ..." Ask yourself these questions:

- Were the majority of the messages you received in childhood positive or negative?

- In what ways were you encouraged to master new skills and achieve new accomplishments?

- In what ways were you discouraged from exploring interests and discovering potential talents?

- What did you tell people you were going to do or be when you grew up?

- What actions earned you acknowledgement or rewards?

- What were you criticized for?

- Did your parents have any unfulfilled dreams? If so, how did their unfulfilled dreams impact you?

Not only do our early experiences shape the messages we play in our heads as adults, but they also shape our assumptions and expectations about the world. These mental assumptions about how the world works are powerful regulators of behavior. Is the world safe or threatening? Can we count on others, or do we need to go it alone? What are the rules of the road, and what happens if we detour from the plan? Is it good to expose our vulnerability to others or more important to maintain a façade of strength and invincibility?

Frederic Hudson, a renowned educator and researcher in adult development, calls these mental assumptions our *internal gyroscope*. Our internal gyroscope, he says, functions as if a committee had meetings in your head to decide what you will do, think, and feel. This committee, made up of parents, siblings, and other significant players, shapes the internal dialogue that decides what we should and shouldn't do, think, and feel, and it assigns blame when we go astray. The childhood years clearly shape, limit, and enrich our adult years. The more we can learn from reevaluating our own childhood, the better we can build fulfilling lives.

Our earliest messages become permanent fixtures in our mind in our adult years unless we consciously choose to change our internal programming of the messages. Exercise 1 will help you reflect on the significant events in your life and how they impact your thinking and behavior.

List the five most significant events in your life.

1. _____

2. _____

3. _____

4. _____

5. _____

Now analyze each significant event according to the following themes. It is possible an event may relate to more than one theme.

1. Does the event mark a major achievement on your part—completing a degree, receiving an award, getting a promotion, winning an athletic event?

2. Does the event reflect a significant loss—the death of a loved one, a romantic relationship gone sour, a financial failure?

3. Does the event relate to adversity, a tragic situation that you or a loved one endured—an automobile crash, a major illness, a natural disaster?

4. Does the event relate to lucky circumstances—winning the lottery, receiving an inheritance?

5. Does the event reflect a major joy in your life—a marriage, the birth of a child, a home renovation?

6. Does the event reflect a major disappointment in yourself or another person—a divorce, an arrest, a job termination?

Now ask yourself how many of the five events that you listed were in the past or will occur in the future. If you are like most people completing this exercise, all of the events you listed were in the past. It is hard to project forward and think in the future tense. But thinking forward and imagining the future we hope to live is what this book is all about. Take this opportunity to list the five most significant events that will take place in your future.

1. _____

2. _____

3. _____

4. _____

5. _____

Getting from Here to There—Themes That Characterize Adulthood

Our lives are never static—we experience each day as a minute increment in our maturational journey through adulthood. Individually, our lives are lived as a series of stories woven across our decade milestones. These stories comprise our unique personal history. Collectively, our stories have helped researchers, psychologists, and adult educators understand the maturational process in adulthood and identify themes and patterns that are universal in nature. Here are a few of the themes that researchers and social scientists have identified.

Context impacts the meaning of events. During the adult years, individuals experience similar developmental tasks and events, such as leaving one's family, choosing an occupation, or establishing long-term relationships, but the meaning of those developmental tasks and events varies considerably. Cultural norms, family history, religious traditions, peer-group influences, gender, and individual needs and dispositions all influence the expectations we have for our lives. Socioeconomic background, geographic location, ethnicity, and political factors also affect the way we interpret and respond to different life events.

Adults view the world through qualitatively different frames of reference as they age. The way we view our family, careers, relationships, and leisure pursuits all modify as we move through adulthood. Many of these changes in perceptions are prompted by our aging bodies—physical changes that force us to slow down, buy reading glasses (or bifocals), and take the elevator instead of the stairs. At each stage we modify our view of the world and of ourselves. Even our concept of job satisfaction changes as we view ourselves differently in our work context. The aging process also changes our perception of time. The restless 20-year-old perceives time as an endless expanse of opportunities compared to 50-year-old, who is more introspective and contemplative.

Adulthood involves an ongoing quest to clarify personal identity. While the seeds of our self-identity are firmly planted in childhood, it does not mean we stop asking the core questions that define us as human beings: Who am I, and what is my purpose on this earth? Questions relating to our self-esteem, our feelings of self-worth, and our sense of autonomy are persistent themes as we age, but the value structures that impact how we answer these questions may change over time.

Healthy adults adapt and grow from life's challenges. Navigating the developmental tasks of adulthood necessitates altering our perceptions of how the world works. It is an ongoing process of retooling the elements of our lives to fit new circumstances. This means adjusting to major personal and professional disappointments and external factors beyond our control. All adults experience a few curve balls—an unforeseen health challenge that requires a lifestyle change, an accident or unexpected natural disaster that wipes out our sense of stability, or the death of a loved one that leaves us shaken and vulnerable. But how we respond to those challenges varies considerably.

Even positive events like winning the lottery require paradigm shifts to accommodate new realities. While we can't control the unexpected challenges that come our way, we do have control over how we choose to respond to those challenges. Healthy adults have developed coping strategies that bolster their sense of resiliency when confronted with adversity.

It's difficult to project into the future. While most people have hopes and dreams for the future, few are able to project a future reality with any degree of precision. Frederic Hudson calls this *future blindness*, our inability to imagine how we will think, feel, and choose to live in the future. Hudson says that particularly when we are young, we project our youthful assumptions, believing that we have sufficient knowledge and power to make the future happen. We believe that our current perspective will suffice to guide us throughout our years; we haven't yet learned that our life orientation changes every decade or so.

If you are in your 50s or older, the truth of this theme is readily apparent. I remember, for example, when I was 30, celebrating my mother's 50th birthday and thinking there was no way that I would ever be that old. I thought that I would defy aging, despite evidence to the contrary. Hudson believes that future blindness serves positive as well as negative functions. It provides a justification for the risk-taking heroic acts that later in life we would probably not undertake with the same degree of certitude and abandon. But even at its best, he believes, future blindness is a form of positive denial about the future.

Adults identify with their peer-group generation. People born in the same decade have a lot in common—major political events that serve as benchmarks for their experiences, movies and music, fashion trends, and social values. These serve as common cultural reference points about the world. Frederic Hudson believes that the critical historical events that occur during our childhoods shape our values and those of our peers throughout the life cycle.

Cohorts who share the same markers in their memories—the Depression, World War II, the civil rights movement, the Vietnam War, the assassinations of JFK and MLK, the Beatles, the end of the Cold War, Bruce Springsteen, hip-hop and rap—view the world through a similar cultural lens. Hudson contends that generational identity has a considerable impact on how we see our lives and the world, which leads to how we age and develop as human beings. The disadvantage of generational identity is that rigid adherence to the values of the past makes adaptation to change difficult.

Maturity begins to grow when you can sense your concern for others outweighing your concern for yourself.

John MacNaughton

Life involves a series of trade-offs. Throughout the adult years we make decisions that involve small and large trade-offs. Some women, for example, decide to forgo having children to pursue their careers. Others opt to stay home and raise a family, putting career and professional pursuits on the backburner. In making decisions about jobs, some individuals take positions with lower pay but better job security. Others decide to endure long daily commutes so they can live in the suburbs. Sometimes the decisions we make regarding trade-offs come with a heavy emotional price—the decision to marry someone of a different race or faith at the risk of alienating our parents, or the decision to leave an abusive relationship at the risk of becoming homeless.

Throughout life we make choices that involve economic, social, and emotional trade-offs. What is important is that we are cognizant of our rationale for the trade-offs we make and clearly understand the pluses and minuses of each option without taking on the guilt of not pursuing the alternative course of action. Think back to the trade-offs that you have made in adulthood relating to relationships, career, family, or self-development. How have they positively or negatively impacted your present situation?

Decade Orientations

While every person's life journey is idiosyncratic and unique, there are predictable chronological stages across our lives. Decade orientations provide indicators of what many in that phase experience. As you read the following descriptions, think about the ways your life mirrors the decade orientation markers described as well as the ways your journey has deviated from these norms.

The 20s. Early adulthood spans the late teens through the 20s. This is the time when individuals consider different options in the world and form an initial perspective of themselves as an independent adult. Leaving home, choosing a career, learning to manage money, and forming a close relationship with a prospective partner are a few of the experiences common in the 20s.

During this decade young adults experiment with a variety of roles and relationships, and their youthful optimism, idealism, energy, and sense of adventure fuel an "anything is possible" attitude. Being inner-directed is a prime concern of young adults in their 20s. This is the decade when individuals sort out the expectations others had for them—their parents, siblings, teachers, and childhood mentors—and make decisions about a path to pursue.

The 30s. The decade of the 30s is the time when many adults settle down and make important decisions about marriage, career, and family. These are weighty decisions that usually involve considerable thinking and discussion about trade-offs—where to work, where to live, when to start a family, how to juggle childrearing commitments, how to achieve financial security. For women, in particular, it is an important decade to sort through all the options relating to making a commitment to a career and the desire to have or not have children. Today, these options have certainly expanded, making individual choice easier about what feels and works best.

Most individuals in their 30s experience a sense of urgency about achieving personal and professional goals. They are driven by an internal press for success in almost every facet of their lives and enjoy recognition for their hard work. Happiness is often defined by the achievement of specific family and career goals and the acquisition of material things.

The 40s. Many looking back on their 40s describe the decade as both the most tumultuous and the most fulfilling time of their lives—a time to take stock of personal relationships and accomplishments, redefine goals, and achieve greater clarity of internal motivations. For many, the decade of the 40s is also a time to move away from needing external rewards and recognition to creating internal markers of success and satisfaction. It is a time to take inventory of one's core values, move toward greater simplicity, and deepen relationships. It is a decade of enormous variation on how these factors play out.

For some, this means reassessing career choices, returning to school, and redirecting efforts in new areas. For others, it means reassessing marital relationships and disrupting family structures. For still others, it means reassessing spiritual connections and creating stronger affiliations with organized religion. As a mid-life transition, the decade of the 40s is important for introspection, self-evaluation, and reflection.

The 50s. For those who successfully navigate life transitions in the 40s, the 50s is a decade of celebration of what one has accomplished and a time to begin to mentor those in younger generations. Leadership responsibilities both at work and in civic and religious organizations are often added to personal agendas. As time spent caring for young children decreases, time for deepening friendships and travel increases.

Many in their 50s take up new hobbies and interests or resurrect past passions that were shelved because of more pressing obligations. Personal health issues may become a focus of attention, and many in their 50s redouble their efforts to lose weight, kick bad habits, and take up more wholesome lifestyles. Health clubs celebrate the half-century marker because those in their 50s are emphatic about staving off the onset of old age by adding a rigorous daily workout to their busy schedules.

The 60s. Many people approach their 60s with a sense of urgency. They know well that time is measured, and they seek ways to maximize living to the fullest.

The middle of your life is an invitation to conscious living.

Oprah Winfrey

The pursuit of personal integrity—living one's values and making the world a better place—are high priorities for those in this decade. But people also approach their 60s with a sense of uncertainty. Issues about personal health, finance, and dealing with aging parents or dependent children are all factors weighing heavily on their minds.

Individuals who enjoy their jobs wonder how long they can continue full-throttle making a valuable contribution to their organizations. Those who are work weary count the days until retirement, but few have actually planned the particulars of their retirement years. This can lead to frustration and regret after the initial euphoria of retirement wears off. The most important ability in the 60s is the capacity to dream and envision what the next twenty years might be if lived fully and intentionally.

The 70s. Today, many in their 70s are fully engaged in careers, volunteer work, or grandparenting. Others are active and thriving in retirement, enjoying the company of friends and family. Regardless of their personal situation, most have accepted the limitations that decreased energy imposes on their capacity to contribute at the same intensity that they had previously.

People in their 70s are intentional; they have little patience for engaging in activities that are not meaningful to them. They have a clear sense of their values and have a broader perspective on life. If their health is stable and strong, they may focus on mentoring, passing on valuable life lessons, and contributing to making the world a better place. Most important, individuals in this decade don't want to be marginalized or discounted as out-of-date or unimportant.

The 80s and 90s. The essence of elderhood in the 80s and 90s is searching for a deeper meaning in life and the legacy one hopes to pass on. The challenge during these decades is to come to terms with one's own mortality, to sustain hope and faith in the face of obstacles and losses, and to feel at peace with the good and not-so-good decisions made during one's lifetime. These decades are about streamlining—reducing one's possessions and external necessities to a minimum. They are also about achieving self-clarity, deepening spiritual commitments, and sharing one's insights and wisdom with others.

The challenge confronting people in their 80s and 90s, of course, is keeping as physically and mentally active as their bodies permit. This means stretching and heart-strengthening exercise despite the aches and pains. It also means infusing as much mental stimulation into daily routines as possible, such as having conversations with grandchildren, doing crossword puzzles, or watching Wheel of Fortune and Jeopardy on television.

We all know people whose life journeys provide colorful exceptions to the decade orientation markers described in this chapter. Women's lives, in particular, are often less linear and more serendipitous than age theories predict. Some women choose not to marry or to marry later in life. Others may have children in their early 20s, while others put off having or adopting children until their 40s or 50s. Nowadays, many grandmothers also find themselves taking on the caretaking responsibility for their grandchildren and attending parent conferences and school functions well into their seventies.

Taking Stock

Author and speaker Christina Baldwin is credited with saying, "How we remember, what we remember, and why we remember form the most personal map of our individuality." Drawing on the wisdom of these words, take some time to reflect on the following:

- How has getting older affected the way you feel about yourself physically, emotionally, spiritually?

- Think of a specific point in time, five, ten, or twenty years ago. What do you know now that you didn't know then? In other words, what are the most valuable lessons life has taught you?

- Is there an older person whose path to maturity has inspired you? Why?

- What are the two dumbest decisions you've made as an adult? What are the life lessons you learned from those decisions?

- Describe a time when you were in the right place at the right time. How did this circumstance impact your life story?

- Think of an important "ah-ha" moment you've experienced in your life. In what way was this experience a turning point in your life, influencing the direction you have taken?

- When was a time you demonstrated great courage in your life?

- When were you most happy in your life?

- When did you experience a low point in your life, a time when you were heavy with grief?

- Who are the two people who have made the greatest positive impact on your life?

The goal in life is to die young—as late as possible.

Ashley Montagu

Thinking in the Future Tense

Virtually all the experts on adult development agree that there is a difference between getting older and aging. Heredity accounts for only one-fourth of the variation in human life spans. It is possible to qualitatively improve our lives as we get older, even as the warranty on our body parts may be ready to expire.

Frederic Hudson encourages people to commit to living to 100 and creating a detailed plan for the rest of their life. Imagining a desirable future, he says, releases your energy and commitment to work toward your goals. Healthy aging includes a positive attitude toward life, good stress-coping skills, health-promoting behaviors, human skills to deal with everyday problems of living, and the good fortune to avoid falling victim to disease or serious injury. Committing to self-renewal means staying at our best—body, mind, and spirit—throughout our life, each and every day.

As I write this chapter, I am caring for Alice, my 99-year-old mother-in-law. She usually resides at an assisted-living facility, but a recent case of the flu took its toll on her, and my husband and I decided our guest bedroom was safer quarters for a few weeks. Alice is still as sharp as a tack, clearly the beneficiary of good genes and a healthy lifestyle. Although her mind is still active, her body is feeling the wear and tear of the decades. She is frail and needs a walker to get around the house, but her strong faith and optimistic spirit have served her well. She has been a wonderful role model for me on aging elegantly. Hats off to you, Alice! I can hardly wait for your 100th birthday.

> *I may not be the man I want to be; I may not be the man I ought to be; I may not be the man I could be; I may not be the man I can be; but praise God, I'm not the man I used to be.*
>
> Martin Luther King Jr.

CHAPTER 3

What Matters Most?

Every once in a while you come across people who truly inspire you. They exude a real enthusiasm for life and a laser-like passion for their work. There is nothing pretentious or contrived about their words or actions. They are the real deal. They know their purpose in life, and they live each day in a manner consistent with their internal gyroscope. I have met several dozen people like this during the course of my life. They represent a full spectrum of roles and occupations including teacher, professor, secretary, artist, accountant, and mechanic. It is not that they are "better" than any of my other friends and colleagues; it is just that I am different when I am in their presence. Their authenticity and their centeredness elevate my expectations for myself. They lift my spirits and inspire me to do better, be better.

There are many questions we ask ourselves in life, but none is more fundamental to our sense of well-being on this planet than "What is my purpose in life?" To answer this question is to confront the very essence of our self-identity. The goal of this chapter is simple: to stop you in your tracks and help you to think deeply about what you value most, to think seriously about what you stand for, and to ask yourself what it would take to be one of those rare people who inspires others to lift their spirits, to do better, to be better.

How Do You Define Success?

The quest for clarity about what matters most necessitates a look at how we define personal success. To be sure, we live in a culture that bombards us with messages about what constitutes success—the size of our paycheck, the balance in our savings account, the label on our jeans, the hood ornament on our car, the awards and recognitions we have received, or the degrees that follow our name. In the end, though, how we define success is a very personal endeavor. For most people, the indicators of success change through the course of adulthood. Definitions of success in our 30s seldom work for us when we are in our 50s.

In his book *Ready for Anything*, David Allen talks about a novel way he came to define success in his personal life. He decided that he would measure his progress as a person not by any specific accomplishment or failure, but rather by the percentage of better choices he made over time. He vows each year to live a year of better choices. Not a bad indicator of success. So what is your yardstick for measuring success in your life?

Determining personal success begins with an assessment of what you want to *have*, what you want to *do*, and what you want to *be* in life.

- **What we have** includes our material possessions—our house, appliances, car, clothes, electronic gadgets, or stocks and bonds.

- **What we do** includes all our activities and accomplishments—our certificates and degrees, work-related responsibilities, roles in the community, actions as a parent and partner, and good deeds to make the world a better place.

- **Who we are** includes our inner-self—our soul, purpose, passion, and personal values.

Most peoples' definition of success is limited to the first two categories. Some devote a lifetime to accumulating material possessions that provide status and recognition. Others are more action-oriented, directing their energies toward achieving accomplishments related to work, family, faith, and community.

Having and doing are important components of one's life, but we also need to attend to our inner-self, setting personal internal standards we want to achieve relating to our purpose, passion, and values. When we aspire to show more patience, love, compassion, or other qualities that we deem important, then we are attending to the inner core of our being. In the end, true success is the alignment between these three areas—when our purpose, passion, and values provide the benchmarks by which to evaluate what we do and what we have.

In his book *Don't Sweat the Small Stuff ... and It's All Small Stuff*, author Richard Carlson challenges readers to redefine *meaningful accomplishment*. He says if you ask the average person what constitutes a meaningful accomplishment, the typical response almost always focuses on things that happen outside of him or herself. Carlson invites readers to think about ways they can measure success from the inside out. For example,

- A friend and I had an argument. I was able to see my friend's point of view.

- A friend recently bought a new car. I was happy for her and did not feel jealous.

- A group project I worked on was a big success. I enjoyed the group's success and did not call attention to my own contributions.

- A friend came to me with a problem. Instead of sharing my problems in return, I simply listened compassionately.

- I woke up one morning in a really bad mood but was able to change my mood so it didn't ruin my day.

How we define success certainly impacts feelings of personal happiness. How often do you catch yourself saying, "I'd be happier if ..." The reality is that most people lead lives built on contingency. They postpone happiness, telling themselves they'll be happy once the car is paid off, they graduate from college, get a promotion, or lose weight. They link happiness to a particular goal or outcome, not the process of achieving that goal. But it is the process of accomplishment that gives meaning to life. The truth is, life will always present us with contingencies if we allow it. We can be happy right now if we learn to value the process as much as the outcome and celebrate the small steps we take toward our goals and accomplishments.

Noted philosopher and psychoanalyst Erich Fromm said that most people spend their lives trying to have enough money so they can do what they want so they can be happy. The trouble is that we get trapped in the first step, never getting enough. In his life Fromm counseled people to turn the equation around. He said, first we need to know who we are, our purpose in life. That will lead us to do what we love. That will then provide clarity about those things we need to have to feel fulfilled.

Digging Deep—Clarifying Values

Every day we make hundreds of decisions—to buy an I-Pod or new tires for the car, to work late or spend the evening with our family, to go to Hawaii on vacation or save for a down payment on a house. In many ways our character, and sometimes our reputation, is defined by the choices we make, either consciously or unconsciously. But our decisions are not random; they are based on our core values and beliefs about what is important and our understanding about how the world works.

A value is a deeply held and enduring view of what we believe to be important and worthwhile. *Adventure, altruism, cooperation, creativity, excellence, family, friendship, honesty, personal growth, prestige, security, social justice*, and *tradition* are just a few of the many values that people embrace as defining aspects of their character. Our core values cut across all facets of our lives. They serve as points of reference, a kind of moral compass for making daily decisions.

Values give rise to our fundamental commitments, the things in life that we consider worthy for their own sake. Our personal values shape our beliefs about what is important to pursue, how we treat others, and how we choose to spend our time. Our values do not usually change drastically throughout our life. They act as a defining anchor but may be expressed differently through adulthood as our life circumstances change.

What are your core values? Our values are shaped by our family upbringing and cultural background as well as our personal experiences, education, and societal influences. Think about the *shoulds* and *should nots* that were loud messages you got as a child, teen, and young adult from your parents, extended family, teachers, and mentors. Reflect also on some of the sayings or expressions you heard repeatedly as a child. Perhaps in your home you heard one or more of these expressions:

- Never put off until tomorrow what you can do today
- A penny saved is a penny earned
- You get out of life what you put into it
- All's fair in love and war
- It's nice to be important, but it's more important to be nice
- Haste makes waste
- If at first you don't succeed, try and try again
- Money doesn't grow on trees
- Truth is mightier than the sword
- The sky is the limit

What other expressions or truisms were part of your upbringing? In what ways did these favorite expressions reinforce certain values or serve to encourage or limit specific behaviors?

Your values and beliefs make you a unique thinking, feeling, and acting human being different from every other person on the planet. Understanding your values and beliefs is at the core of self-awareness and is essential for being an effective early childhood educator.

Take a moment to think about the five most important values that define you as a person and guide your decision making and actions. Next to each value, write your definition of what the value means to you or describe a behavior that demonstrates how you live this value in your personal and professional life.

	Value	*Definition or description of behavior*
1.	_____	_____
2.	_____	_____
3.	_____	_____
4.	_____	_____
5.	_____	_____

Defining the behaviors and actions that exemplify your core values is important because even among commonly identified values, there is wide interpretation of what they mean in action. Let me give an example. I have two dear friends who I am certain would list *family* as one of their core values. I am also certain that the definitions they would use to describe *family* would be quite different. One of my friends is a lesbian, deeply committed to her life partner and raising their young daughter. Her definition of *family* includes embracing alternative family structures relating to gay and lesbian lifestyles. My other friend, very conservative by nature, also believes strongly in *family*. She has put her own career on hold so she can home school her children. Although these two friends both embrace *family* as one of their core values, the way they define and put that value into action daily in the decisions they make is quite different.

Another way to surface your core values is to reflect on the way you respond to questions that target your inner preferences and ideals. Our instinctive, on-the-spot responses to important issues that we feel strongly about often touch a nerve. Complete the following sentences. As you do, think about how your responses reflect your core values.

- My community would be better if ...

- I feel like an outsider when ...

- If I won the lottery, I would ...

- On vacations, I like to ...

- I trust people who ...

- I get angry when ...

- I often feel uncomfortable around people who ...

- I wear my hair the way I do because ...

- It makes me most uncomfortable when ...

- You can count on me to ...

- I am proud to be ...

- The most important thing in life is ...

- I am attracted to people who ...

- I wish the President would ...

Espoused values versus values in action. The Quaker saying, "Let your life speak," captures the admonishment that it is more important to live one's faith than to preach it. How about you? Does your rhetoric match your actions? Are there core values you listed in the exercise earlier that you believe are important but are not lived fully in your daily interactions and routines?

As humans, we often contradict ourselves. We know the socially desirable response we should make or the values we hope to aspire to, but we often fall short of living those values fully. We say one thing and we do another. We say we value teamwork and accountability but put things off until the last minute, causing stress for our colleagues when deadlines aren't met. We say we value health and self-discipline but continue to overindulge in unhealthy foods, putting our physical well-being at risk.

Looking at the alignment between your espoused values versus your values-in-action is not a one-time endeavor. It should be an ongoing process, an essential component of living from the inside out. Conducting a personal audit of how you allocate your time is one simple way to see how well your behavior matches your espoused values. Take a few minutes to complete Exercises 3.

Unless you're in prison under lock and key, you probably have the freedom to make decisions about how to spend the 168 hours you have been granted each week. Think about your typical week and how much time you spend in activities and responsibilities related to your different roles. Note the total weekly time in the space provided. Cross off a category if it doesn't apply to you or add one that may be more appropriate.

_____ Work (paid employment)

_____ Commuting to and from work

_____ Entertainment (dining out, going to movies and theatre, attending sports and social events)

_____ Errands (shopping for groceries, dropping off the dry cleaning, mailing packages)

_____ Fitness (at home, around the block, or at the club)

_____ Health (doctor visits, therapy)

_____ Hobbies

_____ Housekeeping (cooking, laundry, cleaning)

_____ Leisure (watching television, browsing the Internet, reading)

_____ Parenting (helping with homework, chauffeuring children, attending school events)

_____ Professional development (attending classes or in-service training, professional reading)

_____ Sleep and romance

_____ Spiritual renewal (prayer, meditation, journal writing, religious events)

_____ Volunteer work (church, community, civic organizations)

168 total hours

How we spend our hard-earned cash also provides clues as to what we value in our lives. Some people save for exotic vacations and enjoy traveling to different parts of the globe; others dine out regularly, join a health club, get weekly manicures, or buy fashionable clothes or jewelry. Think about those scrimp and splurge categories in your own life and whether or not they reflect the values you noted earlier.

When values conflict. Knowing if your espoused values match your values in action is certainly important, but sometimes the struggle we face as adults is not so much a matter of doing what is right as choosing between two rights. Much of the internal stress people feel occurs when their priorities pull them in different directions:

- *Do I study for my college class this evening (personal growth) or help my son with his homework (commitment to family)?*

- *Do I express how I really feel about a colleague's proposal during a meeting (honesty) or keep my thoughts to myself and go along with the group (cooperation and teamwork)?*

- *Do I volunteer at the soup kitchen at my church on Saturday (social justice) or go to my daughter's piano recital (commitment to family)?*

These kinds of internal debates are not easily resolved. Being aware of the trade-offs we are sometimes forced to make, though, is important for understanding why we may be experiencing emotional turmoil.

Value conflicts are also at the heart of the interpersonal tensions we experience in our lives. It is easy to solve disputes with others when the issue has to do with facts and data. It is when the issue revolves around competing core values that our emotions can hijack reason. Just think of the heated debates on issues like women's reproductive rights, stem cell research, or the death penalty. When deeply felt values clash, interpersonal relations can't help but be strained.

Beliefs and Assumptions

A belief is somewhat different from a value. It is our personal conviction that certain things are true or that certain statements are facts. Our beliefs are the lens through which we view the world. They form the mental models that give focus and clarity to our interpretation of the world.

Our connection to work as early childhood educators relies on two kinds of beliefs. First, there are beliefs about ourselves. These are our personal expectations about our capabilities, the kind of people we aspire to be, and how we should act in different situations. These beliefs can be positive or negative, accurate or inaccurate. They are what they are—strong forces shaping our potential and self-efficacy expectations. The things we believe and expect of ourselves in large part determine what we are able to do. Negative, limiting beliefs erode our motivation and faith in our ability to accomplish what we want.

There are also our beliefs about the important work we do—educating young children and their families. Many of these beliefs center on the nature of learning and teaching. Teachers' implicit beliefs guide their expectations about child behavior and the decisions they make in classrooms every day. For example, if teachers believe that the causes of student learning and success lie largely outside the school, in a child's genetic makeup or the social background of a family, then they may feel that their potential impact is limited. If on the other hand, teachers believe that achievement is the product more of a child's effort than the child's innate talent, then they are more likely to embrace the notion that their efforts can make big difference.

So what do you believe? What do you feel most passionate about? What makes your heart sing? What makes your blood boil? Think about your deepest beliefs as you complete these sentences:

- I believe the world would be a better place if ...

- I believe that children should ...

- I believe everyone has the right to ...

- I believe that if I really wanted to, I could...

- I believe the one thing holding me back in life is ...

- I believe someday I might ...

- I believe more people should ...

- I believe in ...

What Is Your Calling?

I don't know about you, but I am a real Oprah fan. The thing that I admire most about this amazing woman is her unbridled passion for her work. Regardless of what scorecard you use, she has succeeded in some amazing accomplishments—from encouraging reading through her book club to helping victims of Katrina reclaim their lives through her Angel Network. Despite a litany of good deeds, it was her supreme moment of destiny, she says, when she realized her true calling—to educate young girls in South Africa, bringing hope and opportunity by creating the Oprah Winfrey Leadership Academy for Girls.

> The two most important times in our lives are when we are born and when we find out why we were born.
>
> *Farah Gray*

People who love life and love what they do, day in and day out, are quick to respond when asked to talk about their passions. They know their purpose in life; they don't need prompting and they don't say, "Let me get back to you tomorrow; I need to think about that for a while." They know what fuels their spirit.

One way to think about your purpose in life is to think about your legacy. How is it that you want to be remembered? In his book *What is Your Life's Work?*, Bill Jensen encourages people to write legacy letters. Imagine, he says, having a profound, plain-spoken conversation with your loved ones. You speak with absolute conviction: "This is what I stood for, believed in, struggled with, and accomplished. This is my life's work, and what I want to be remembered for."

Our purpose is that which we strive for or a goal we seek to fulfill. It is the result of our efforts, our best intentions. That is not to say that one's calling is static or never changes as life circumstances change; but it does mean that one's calling must come from within. We can't live out someone else's agenda. This means learning to trust our own intuition and our own perceptions about what feels right and good for us.

This is really hard for many adults who have shaped their self-esteem on other people's judgments. Not surprising, of course. From our earliest years we hear praise from family and teachers that makes us rely heavily on their assessment of the value of our efforts. We hear, "That's a good drawing; you make me so proud" rather than "You worked really hard on that drawing; it must make you feel really proud." Even as a college professor, I am struck how uncomfortable many students feel when I ask them to evaluate the quality of their own work and assign a grade assessing their efforts. They are more interested in knowing how I view their performance than undertaking the uncomfortable task of assessing their own efforts.

As the story goes, the brilliant Buckminster Fuller, the inventor of the geodesic dome, fell into a deep depression after a business failure. He contemplated suicide. Instead of ending his life, however, Fuller chose to live, but to live consciously as though each day was a precious gift. Each new day he would ask himself, "What is it on this planet that needs doing that I know something about, that probably won't happen unless I take responsibility for it?" So ask yourself, what is your job on this planet?

- What deserves your precious 1,440 minutes each day?

- Does your life's work energize you?

- What price are you willing to pay for what matters most to you?

- Is anything important missing from your life right now?

Thinking about and gaining clarity about one's calling or purpose in life is in essence a spiritual act. It is what connects our inner and outer lives. In the Hindu and Buddhist traditions, the term *karma* describes the sum of all that an individual has done, is currently doing, and will do. Karma means that this happens because that happened. Every effort has an antecedent cause, and every cause an effect. The effects of all deeds by an individual are responsible for past, present, and future experiences, thus making one responsible for one's own life and the pain and joy it brings to others.

exercise 4

This is your opportunity to weave together your thoughts about how you put your values into action. First, think about your different roles in life—wife/husband, mother/father, daughter/son, sibling, friend, center director, advocate, church member, community volunteer, dog trainer, antique collector. What are your true passions related to these different roles? What is your purpose in life related to these different roles? What do you want to be, to do, and to have related to these different roles?

My roles in life:

_____   _____

_____   _____

_____   _____

My true passions:

_____

_____

_____

My purpose in life:

_____

_____

_____

What I want to be—the qualities I want to be known for:

_____

_____

_____

What I want to do—the accomplishments I hope to achieve:

_____

_____

_____

What I want to have—the tangible material possessions I hope to acquire:

_____

_____

_____

The legacy I hope to leave:

_____

_____

_____

> *To leave the world a bit better, whether by a healthy child, a garden patch, or a redeemed social condition; to know that even one life has breathed easier because you lived—that is to have succeeded.*
>
> Ralph Waldo Emerson

CHAPTER 4

Becoming a Director—Intention or Improvisation

Several years ago a cartoon appeared in the *San Francisco Chronicle* depicting an inquiring reporter asking a young woman why she wanted to become a mortician. "Because," she said, "I enjoy working with people." Reading that cartoon sent me into hoots of laughter. At the time, I was directing an early childhood program. Just the day before, I had participated on a panel discussing the joys and frustrations of administering a preschool before an audience of high school seniors considering career options. One young woman in the audience had asked me why I decided to become a director, and, as you can guess, I replied, "Because I enjoy working with people."

Like many in our field, I arrived at early childhood education through the back door, as a result of serendipitous events rather than a carefully thought-out career plan. And like many who enter early childhood education, I was idealistic and eager to improve conditions for young children. This chapter will ask you to step back and reflect on the career decisions you've made that have led you to where you are today. It will give you a framework for understanding the growth and development of director competence through the career cycle. You'll draw on this self-knowledge in later chapters as you make some bold decisions about the next steps in your career.

Directors' Career Decisions

In her book *Composing a Life*, Mary Catherine Bateson proposes that the act of composing our lives is oftentimes improvisation—that we discover the shape of our creation along the way, rather than pursuing a vision already defined. That is clearly the case for many early childhood directors, including myself. In the research I've conducted on this topic, I've found that less than one-fifth of directors report that they always knew they wanted to become a center director and actively pursued the role. In response to how they reached their current position, the largest percentage of directors indicate that others saw their leadership ability and encouraged them (even coaxed and persuaded them) to take the position.

The lack of a focused career path leading to a director's office is not surprising given that the field of early childhood lacks a well-articulated career lattice or an established pattern of mentor relationships to provide guidance for those at different points in their careers. Approximately 90 percent of the directors surveyed report that they were teachers before assuming their first directorship, but few report that they had any formal administrative training prior to beginning their jobs as directors.

For many, their own experience—learning while doing—is the most relied-upon source for acquiring management knowledge and skills. Only one-third of early childhood administrators report they felt confident and self-assured when they first became a director. More than three-quarters indicate they were not prepared for the kinds of issues they encountered.

Take a moment now to reflect back on your own career path and your decision to become an early childhood administrator:

- What individuals or events in your life were instrumental in your decision to become a director?

- Did your initial impression and understanding of the role match the reality?

- Did your experience and training adequately prepare you for the scope of responsibilities required of your position?

- Would you choose a career in early childhood education again if you could retrace your steps and make new decisions about your education and career prospects?

Learning the Ropes

In research I conducted a few years ago on directors' career decisions, I interviewed a young woman named Deborah who had recently been hired as the director of a large child care center. Her center was part of an established social service agency. In her new role, Deborah functioned as a "middle manager." She supervised a staff of 30 and reported to the agency's director of educational programs.

When I asked Deborah how she would characterize her first six months on the job, she replied, "This has been a slow process of learning what ropes to pull and what ropes to jump." Her remark got me thinking about how directors are socialized into their jobs, particularly when they are caught in the middle, being tugged by demands from above as well as below.

Job socialization describes how individuals adapt to their roles—how they act on their beliefs and values and learn to accommodate the beliefs and values of others. As directors mature in professional competence, the kinds of social strategies they use to conform to different organizational and institutional demands goes through a subtle transformation. I believe four stages describe the thought patterns and belief systems of directors who work in an organizational context where they are middle managers reporting to a corporate office, a board of directors, or an agency executive director.

Blind compliance. Blind compliance is when a director complies with an authority figure's definition of a situation and believes this conformity to be for the best. Individuals at this stage are willing to develop into the kind of person the situation demands. Listen to Connie as she reflects on her career:

> *When I first began as director, the agency CEO installed a punch clock for employees. He said it was necessary to keep people honest. He also suggested I prohibit teachers from using the office telephone and instead make them use the pay phone in the building next door if they wanted to make an outgoing call. I never questioned the wisdom of his suggestions. I just assumed his management philosophy was correct; after all, he was so much older and more experienced than I was. Now I look back and laugh. I was such an amoeba then, so obedient and compliant.*

Uncomfortable compliance. This is when the director complies with the constraints posed by a situation but retains private reservations about doing so. Individuals at this stage do not act in ways consistent with their underlying beliefs; their outward conformity is an adaptive response without the corresponding personal value commitment.

Many of the ethical dilemmas directors face reflect this kind of response. For example, some directors comply with the demands of a board or owner to cut corners on quality. They will over-enroll classes, deny staff their entitled breaks, and even limit purchases of basic supplies essential for program functioning. They comply because they are intimidated by their superiors or fearful of the consequences of insubordination. They know their actions don't match their beliefs, but they comply nevertheless. As one director expressed,

> *I find myself purchasing more and more workbooks for the pre-kindergarten group because the board and parents want tangible proof that the children are "learning" something at school. I don't really feel this is the best way for children to learn, but I want to keep the parents happy.*

Working the system. In this stage a director makes changes or maneuvers around organizational constraints without the formal power to do so. Individuals in this response mode know how to cut through red tape and make things happen without being cast as a rebel. Letitia's story reflects this strategy:

My agency had this ridiculous rule that no one could be in the building unless the custodian was also on the premises. In fact, the custodian had the only key to the building. The rule was implemented as a security measure. I know the intent was good, but it really clashed with my work style. I like to do my paperwork after the center closes in the evening and I like to come in on weekends to work on the bulletin boards. I quickly learned how to get around the system. Once a week I bought pizza for the custodian. I also rented videos for him. Since he was a widower and had no one to go home to, the arrangement worked great. I got my work done; he got a free dinner and entertainment.

Redefining the system. This final stage is when a director is able to educate and persuade a supervisor, board, or agency executive director into adopting new ways of thinking about organizational issues and perceived constraints. These individuals are adept at advocating for needed changes to make their programs more efficient and effective.

Kathy, the director of a large United Way program, is one such director. Over the past few years, as her program has grown, so too have the demands on her time. Kathy realized that if she was to maintain the high quality of her program, she needed to hire an assistant director. Her agency's board, faced with other fiscal challenges, did not want to create a new position.

In a nonadversarial way, Kathy was able to work with her board to come up with a creative win/win strategy to achieve her goal of increased staffing. She wrote a proposal and received a grant from a local corporation to buy educational materials. This freed up funds in the instructional supplies line item of her budget that she shifted to the personnel line item of her budget. She then persuaded her board to modify the agency's policy so she could rent out a large gym to different community groups on the weekend. The income generated from these two strategies was sufficient for her board to fund a new assistant director position.

It is clear from the directors I have interviewed that being a middle manager presents many challenges. Directors in the middle need to establish their own identity, yet they must remain accountable to those to whom they report. Role ambiguity fueled by divided loyalties creates its own special type of job stress. Deborah described her job socialization as learning which ropes to jump and which to pull. Perhaps, like a circus performer, being a middle manager is also like performing a balancing act on a tight-rope connecting two worlds with differing demands and expectations.

Defining Director Competence

Anyone who has chased a director's shadow for even a brief time knows that being an effective administrator means wearing many hats—from budget analyst to nutritionist to fundraiser. The list is long and varied. Defining competence as it relates to the multiplicity of roles the director assumes each day is a thorny task. It is thorny because we as a profession have not defined precisely what we mean by the terms *competence*, *competent*, and *competency*. These terms are overused and misused in our well-intentioned attempts to improve educational practice.

Many educators embrace a definition of competence as "the ability to do the right thing, at the right time, for the right reasons." Though appealing, the problem with such a definition is that it rests on qualitative judgments that are value laden. The *right thing* or the *right reasons* are highly subjective terms open to multiple interpretations. How does one begin to measure competence using this kind of yardstick?

Competence is clearly context-specific. The repertoire of competencies needed to effectively carry out the administrator's role varies by the age and background of the children enrolled, the range of services provided, the philosophical orientation of the program, and the legal sponsorship of the center. The size of the program, as well, certainly affects the scope and complexity of the administrative role. Directors of small programs may have fewer administrative demands and serve as classroom teacher for part of the day, whereas directors of large programs may have multiple sites, multiple funding sources, and a large, diverse staff to coordinate. Thus, directing different types of programs requires varying levels of administrative sophistication.

Another problem with current discussions of director competence is that they tend to frame the issue in either/or, dichotomous terms. But competence isn't like the chicken pox—either you have it or you don't. Rather, proficiency in different competencies needs to be viewed on a continuum. A director may be highly proficient in one area but only moderately so in another.

Despite the difficulty in achieving clarity on the specific administrator competencies needed for different types of programs, most leaders in the field do agree that any conceptualization of competence needs to include three components:

- **knowledge competency**—this includes knowledge in such areas as child development, leadership and management practices, group dynamics, organizational theory, teaching strategies, and family systems;

- **skill competency**—this includes the technical, human, and conceptual skills needed to perform different tasks like developing a budget, motivating staff, solving problems; and

- **attitude competency** this includes beliefs, values, dispositions, and emotional responses that support optimum performance.

There are people who will act on Monday in their job based on experiences they had in the third grade.

Michael Brandwein

Since most directors have been classroom teachers, they come to their administrative positions with a basic understanding of the fundamentals of child development and early childhood curriculum. But as a director, you know firsthand that a strong background in theory and practice of early childhood is not enough. Effective administration of a center-based program also necessitates a strong grasp of basic business and management knowledge and skill in applying those principles as a leader in your organization.

Appendix A delineates the competencies identified for effective program administration. As you read through each competency area, make notes in the margins about your level of proficiency in each area. In a later chapter you'll have a chance to develop a plan for adding to your repertoire of knowledge and skills by strengthening those areas you've noted.

Directors' Developmental Stages

No early childhood administrator walks into the director's office feeling totally confident and capable the first day on the job. Administering an early childhood program is a complex process in which competence is achieved over time. Even directors who have a degree in child development and early childhood program administration grow into their positions gradually, achieving a sense of confidence and competence.

Competence can be framed as a developmental progression, from novice director to capable director to master director. In my research, I have found that approximately 30 percent of administrators describe themselves as novice directors; 60 percent fit into the capable director category; and only 10 percent believe they are master directors.

The novice director. The novice director is filled with excitement and anticipation, eager to make a meaningful contribution. That excitement, however, is coupled with anxiety. Many directors in this category identify with the term *reality shock* in describing their reactions as they assume their first administrative position. Several circumstances surprise them: the emotional and physical stamina required of the job, the amount of paperwork, the range and intensity of staff's and parents' needs, and the lack of support they often get from their center's administrative board or agency. One director, Crystal, now in her fourth year administering a program, reflects on her first year:

> *I dreamed of the day I would be a director—to be the one "in charge." I really thought I was well prepared for the position. How naïve I was! I really didn't have a clue about so many things. I survived that first year because of sheer determination, not because I was the least bit competent.*

The picture Crystal describes fits into the *unconscious incompetence* learning stage described in Chapter 1. She didn't even know what she didn't know. This is one reason why needs assessments for novice directors are not very valuable. An individual needs a base of experience to understand the knowledge and skill areas that need to be mastered. As novice directors build a base of administrative competence during their first and second years on the job, they quickly move into the learning stage of *conscious incompetence*—being keenly aware of all there is yet to learn about the demands of the job.

Despite the need for guided entry into the administrative role, the sink-or-swim method of induction seems to prevail. One director notes, "I didn't know the difference between a debit or a credit, yet I was responsible for a half-million-dollar operating budget that first year." Few states require any specialized training in management as a prerequisite for the director role. Most early childhood center directors are selected because of exemplary performance as classroom teachers, not because they have demonstrated competence in administration.

Novice directors often express intense concern about their feelings of adequacy, their ability to handle the managerial demands of the job, and their desire to be liked and appreciated by staff and families. They also have concerns about the quality and impact of their program; but when these concerns are probed more deeply, they are usually couched in language relating to their own need to be validated, to be told they are doing a good job.

Some directors who have been promoted from within talk about the instant isolation they experience when they assume their administrative role. As one director states,

> *All of a sudden I was the enemy; no longer was I one of the group. It upset me so much when I walked into the kitchen on my third day as director and three teachers stopped talking. It really hurt.*

These feelings are disconcerting to the novice director who wants desperately to be liked. It appears that these feelings are not unique to early childhood administration. Elementary and secondary school principals experience similar misgivings about their capacity to fulfill their roles and their need to be accepted.

Many, but not all, novice directors have a survival focus—a concern with "just making it." These directors may be so preoccupied with whether they are personally up to meeting the multiple demands confronting them each day that they are unable to see beyond the immediate exigencies. Many novice directors are also concerned about status—their personal status in the organization and their status in the field.

The relationships we have with the world are largely determined by the relationships we have with ourselves.

Greg Anderson

The reason that a survival focus and concerns about status do not uniformly describe all novice directors is that many individuals moving into program administration are in their thirties or forties. The range of life experiences and the greater sense of self-assurance that accompanies adult development may temper some of the insecurities that characterize the novice director who is in his or her twenties.

The capable director. The capable director emerges after a period of competency building between one and four years into the job. Somewhere in this period the individual makes a subtle but important shift from *struggling* to *juggling*. The capable director is no longer concerned about merely coping. Rather, concerns seem to center on time (being able to accomplish all that needs to be done) and on meeting expectations (both externally and internally imposed). In other words, capable directors are not concerned about whether or not they can accomplish the wide range of tasks demanded of them; they worry about how they can do them better.

The capable director has come to terms with two myths in program administration—that directors will be liked by everyone and that one right answer exists for every issue. They have also accepted the reality that hard work often goes unappreciated and that the qualities that made them a superstar teacher are not necessarily the same qualities that will make them a successful director.

Capable directors fit into the learning stage of *conscious competence*. They are analytic, consciously monitoring their thoughts and actions, making strategic decisions thoughtfully. They have the metacognitive ability to stand back and reflect on how they are doing while they are doing. Balance seems to be a key issue for capable directors—balance between personal and professional obligations, balance between the people and the paper demands of the job, and balance between meeting the needs of individuals and those of the organization.

The master director. This final developmental stage describes a small percentage of experienced directors who have moved to a higher level of reflection and competence in their administrative roles. These directors still worry about how they are going to juggle the multiple demands of their jobs, but they don't seem to dwell on the stressful aspects of their role. Master directors are able to describe their centers from a systems perspective; they understand the nature of organizational change and the importance of their role as change agent. They are confident in their ability to handle virtually any curve ball thrown their way.

Master directors describe themselves most often as role models, advocates, mentors, or leaders. They are in the *unconscious competence* stage, performing at a high level without having to analyze every thought and action. They are on automatic pilot, making subtle, spontaneous adjustments in behavior as the situation dictates. They understand themselves well—their emotions and defense mechanisms as well as their cognitive strengths and weaknesses. The examples they give regarding administrative decision making clearly illustrate *affective neutrality*, the ability to work with staff, parents, and the center's board with objectivity and tempered emotional involvement.

Master directors seem comfortable and confident in their personal leadership style. Many describe their conscious attempt to balance activities that require gathering, sharing, and analyzing information in linear ways (yang) with activities that involve creativity, emotional expression, and personal insight (yin). Most important, they have developed a clear sense about role expectations and are able to communicate to their coworkers how they perceive the scope and nature of their administrative role so that role expectations are more compatible.

Master directors seldom talk in absolutes or look for quick-fix solutions to problems; rather, they understand that most issues surfacing in early childhood program administration are complex and can be viewed from multiple perspectives. They challenge the status quo by looking for new ways to solve old problems. They have the capacity for critical thinking—the ability to make a judgment and then qualitatively explain or defend that judgment.

Master directors see themselves as mentors to their teachers and to other directors. They see the connection between the developmental concepts and instructional strategies used with children and their work with adults. As Virginia, an 11-year veteran of an NAEYC-accredited program, states, "I look for those teachable moments with my staff, an opportunity to scaffold their understanding of an issue to a higher level of analysis." Master directors are able to articulate their theories and beliefs about leadership, management, and their role in the process of organizational change. They reflect on and analyze the effects of their leadership style and apply the results of these reflections to future actions.

Like novice and capable directors, master directors are also concerned about the diminishing pool of highly qualified staff, about the fact that there are too few hours in the day to do so many things, and about the public's perception of early care and education. They don't perseverate on these issues though, and don't fall into the trap of playing victim. They understand the nature of organizational change and their own role in achieving long-term goals, both for their program and for the field of early childhood. Their primary concern is the impact of their program in the lives of the children and families they serve.

Growth and Change over the Career Cycle

The process of change that characterizes the professional growth and development of individuals, from novice to capable to master director, resembles a spiral moving upward. Each rotation upward is influenced by formal and informal educational opportunities, experience, the context of development, and the sphere of relationships involved. These influences can be family, formal and informal mentors, or other significant individuals who serve to inspire, support, and promote deeper levels of self-awareness during the career cycle.

The progression represents a transformation in the developing administrator that is more complex, however, than the mere accumulation of new knowledge and acquired skills. It represents a positive shift in expectations of self-efficacy, an individual's ability to think more abstractly about issues and events and take alternative points of view, and an increased capacity for introspection.

Exercise 5 provides an opportunity for you to reflect on where you are in your own career cycle and your developmental journey of building competence.

exercise 5

Which developmental stage best describes where you are today—novice, capable, master? What are the challenges you currently face, and what new challenges are you likely to face during the next three years? What supports do you need to have in place to help you progress to a higher level of confidence and competence in your job? If you are in that 10 percent category of master directors, what can you do to mentor and support other novice or capable directors?

_____

_____

_____

_____

_____

_____

> *Every day in the life of a child care center, hassles occur which can discourage even the hardiest of souls. That's why the director needs to be the defender of faith, the bearer of the torch, the dealer in hope.*
>
> Roger Neugebauer

CHAPTER 5

IT FITS! IT FITS!

Maximizing the Fit

Different roles in any organization carry with them associated expectations; both self-expectations and the expectations of others. These role perceptions evolve from a set of beliefs about the workplace and the status and worth of chosen careers. They also tend to reflect an individual's experiences and preferences, culture, level of education, and personal philosophy. So understanding your own role perceptions is essential for maximizing the fit between you and the job you hold and the organization in which you work.

My interest in directors' role perceptions was prompted by an incident a number of years ago, when I was the director of a campus laboratory school. I had just finished giving a new parent a tour of the school. While she completed her enrollment forms, I offered to entertain her son in my office. Jonathan inspected the photographs and plaques on my wall, surveyed the books and knick-knacks on my shelf, and carefully eyed the stack of papers on my desk. He then turned to me and in the unabashed candor so characteristic of a four-year-old said, "You must be the queen of this school." Deciding that a four-year-old wasn't quite ready for a lecture on how "queen" didn't exactly square with my management philosophy, I simply turned to Jonathan and said, "Yes, I guess a director is a lot like a queen."

Jonathan has since graduated from college, but his innocent remark has remained etched in my memory. During these intervening years I've thought a lot about how individuals view their roles and the power that personal perceptions have in shaping one's professional identity. In this chapter you will have the opportunity to examine your internal perceptions of your role and the factors impacting your level of job satisfaction and professional fulfillment.

The Power of Metaphors

A metaphor links an idea or concept to a visual representation of that idea or concept. "Her degree is her passport to success" and "The teacher's grin was a stamp of approval" are both metaphors. Metaphors are not logical; they label something that it really isn't. By engaging the mind in making translations from word thinking to picture thinking, though, metaphors stimulate new ways of perceiving the ordinary elements of our lives.

I have found that metaphors can be a powerful tool in promoting the personal and professional self-awareness of early childhood directors. This is because the metaphors individuals use often carry with them implicit natural solutions to the personal concerns they may be dealing with. Before continuing on in this chapter, take a moment to think metaphorically about your role and your job by completing Exercise 6.

exercise 6

Think of a metaphor that you believe aptly describes the role of the director. Then think of a metaphor that describes your specific job. You can also use a simile, inserting the word *like*, if that is easier. For example, *Life is like a highway because we cruise along and sometimes we hit a pothole or have to make a detour to get to where we want to go.*

A director is   _____

    because   _____

My job is   _____

    because   _____

In my research on this topic, I have found that when asked to think of a metaphor for their administrative role (*A director is a* ...), individuals tend to select somewhat different images from those they select specifically for their own job (*My job is a* ...). Metaphors regarding their overall administrative role often reflect a set of idealized expectations about their position, their beliefs about the importance of the role, and their summary judgment about the nature of the position. The metaphors directors use to describe their jobs specifically are richly descriptive of the demands they experience every day.

Role. The most dominant theme that surfaces when directors refer to their administrative role is the multifaceted nature of the position, which requires the balancing of multiple tasks and responsibilities. About 40 percent of directors give responses that fit into one of three related categories—balancing, multiple tasks, or balancing multiple tasks and responsibilities. The most frequently mentioned metaphor used is *juggler*.

If you've been a director for more than ten minutes, you'll appreciate the accuracy of this metaphor. Being an effective administrator means juggling many different tasks and responsibilities daily. While administering an early childhood program has never been easy, the director's job has gotten increasingly complex and difficult in recent years; the number of balls to keep up in the air at any one time has multiplied. Listen to Tom, a director for 20 years, as he describes the personal relevance of the juggler metaphor to his professional experience:

> *The director needs to keep his eye on many things at once and hopefully not let too many of them drop, at least not the important things. It's a daily choice which things you're going to deal with. You need to be comfortable with the understanding that you're never going to be able to do everything you need to. There is simply no rest from it—there is always something coming at you.*

Metaphors that describe the leading and guiding functions of the director's role are used by approximately 30 percent of the directors. These metaphors were more varied, however. Individuals used metaphorical references to leadership roles in other fields (orchestra conductor, football coach, safari guide) as well as things that symbolize leadership attributes (lighthouse).

Interestingly, absent from directors' metaphorical references is the theme of exerting power and influence. Leadership is virtually always viewed as guiding, coordinating, inspiring, and motivating; never cajoling, forcing, or imposing. The lack of metaphors connoting power and influence is consistent with previous research that has found that early childhood directors (most of whom are female) have a preference for participatory, nonhierarchical management styles. Many directors even express discomfort when thinking about their role as involving a position of authority.

Two additional metaphorical categories, nurturing/protecting and making connections, merit discussion because they are central to the field of early childhood and to feminist literature. Together, these two categories are mentioned by approximately one-fourth of directors. These are important themes because they provide an explanatory framework for understanding the management philosophy of many early childhood directors as well as many of the role-related stress issues that confront directors.

Job. When directors are asked to use a metaphor to describe their specific job, there is a clear and consistent pattern to their responses. One-half of all responses relate to pace and to dealing with the unexpected. The most frequently cited metaphor combining these two elements is *roller coaster*. Karen, a seasoned director of a large nonprofit center, elaborates on this metaphor.

> *The roller coaster typically has the longest line in the amusement park. Pretend that those waiting in line have never been on a roller coaster. They look up and say, "Why can't those people get control of that ride?" How surprised they are to find out that when they get on the ride, they can't do any better. That's why it's such a wild ride. With maturity you can learn to handle the fast downs. But a director in the survival stage is in the last car getting whipped around. You don't really get off until you leave your program.*

> I'm in a job where people are fighting to make my in-box interesting.
>
> *Jim Levine*

The Discrepancy between Current and Ideal

When directors reflect on the subtext and personal meanings associated with metaphor choices, their analysis often highlights the discrepancy between the current and the ideal perceptions of their role. If directors have expectations, for example, that they should be like the captain of a jumbo jet or the head coach for a Super Bowl team, and yet the reality of their everyday life is more like a Ferris wheel spinning nonstop or a doormat that everyone walks all over, that discrepancy can lead to role stress and feelings of inadequacy.

The in-depth conversations that I've had with directors reveal that most directors experience conflicting emotions about their jobs. On the one hand, they derive enormous satisfaction and personal rewards from serving children and families. They appreciate the diversity of their tasks, the opportunity to solve complex problems, and the chance to learn more about their own abilities and beliefs. At the same time, however, they experience enormous frustration about not being able to meet everyone's needs and not having enough time and energy to achieve their dream of operating a smoothly functioning, crisis-free program.

Marlene, the director of a small for-profit center, is typical of many directors with whom I have worked over the years. She states, "My greatest satisfaction is the smile on parents' faces when their children tell them all the wonderful things they did during the course of the day." When asked to describe her frustrations on the job, she pours out a litany of complaints about parents who don't comply with the center's policies, parents who don't follow through with their commitments, and parents who are neglectful of their basic parenting responsibilities. Parents are the source of her greatest satisfaction yet also the source of her deepest frustrations.

When asked to describe the role of the director in metaphorical terms, Marlene used the metaphor of an orchestra conductor: "The good conductor is 'in charge' and knows how to achieve real harmony out of very different (and sometimes competing) sounds." This metaphor captured Marlene's idealized expectations for herself as a director, that she should be able to achieve perfect harmony out of all the competing needs at her center. In sharp contrast was the metaphor she used to describe her specific job: "I'm like a marionette. Everyone pulls my strings. They can make me jump, hop, and dance, even when I don't want to."

A common theme expressed by many directors is that they are expected to be all things to all people. Certainly Marlene's metaphor about her job captures elements of this theme. A primary organizing principle for women's lives is "doing for others." Many women define themselves as moral agents in terms of their capacity to care. Thus their sense of self-worth is often tied to how much they give to others. The result of this orientation is that many women put their own needs at the bottom of the list after children, staff, and family members—even to the point of depletion.

Diane, the director of a half-day preschool program, offers this metaphor: "I'm an ATM machine—I'm always ready to give different amounts of time, energy, and care to different people at a moment's notice." Her ATM metaphor captures the essence of the caring/nurturing role perception expressed by many directors.

After sharing Diane's metaphor with a group of directors, I asked them to come up with creative strategies that a director could use to reduce role stress. They were quick to offer advice. "The ATM machine could give out smaller bills." "How about posting an Out of Order sign and directing people to another ATM machine?" "I'd increase the service charge for using the ATM machine." "The bank should let customers know they also need to make deposits to the ATM machine." After generating a dozen or so creative ideas like this, it doesn't take much to translate each of these metaphorical solutions into concrete practical strategies that directors can use to put the ever-pressing demands of their jobs in perspective.

Now look again at the two metaphors that you used to capture the director's role and your own job in Exercise 6. Do they reflect a discrepancy between your idealized notion of what the position should be and the day-to-day realities of your experience? If so, what metaphorical and real solutions can you come up with to reduce that discrepancy?

Sources of Satisfaction and Frustration

To be sure, jobs differ in their demands and opportunities, and people differ in their needs and abilities. As organizational theorist Daniel Katz says, the interaction of work and the worker poses a kind of societal paradox; we create social institutions and we are in turn created by them. Job satisfaction has everything to do with the goodness of fit between the individual and the organization.

When the values, needs, expectations, and skills of an individual match the expectations and requirements of the job, it is like two pieces of a puzzle that fit together tightly. Job satisfaction and fulfillment are high. However, when a puzzle piece does not fit the open spot, job stress may result. That is why two teachers who do essentially the same work can have such contrasting perceptions about their jobs. One will complain and grumble about the children's behavior, the assigned responsibilities, and the perceived lack of support while the other is energized by the daily routine, finding purpose and passion in the work assigned.

On an abstract level we can think of job satisfaction as the degree to which our work matches our ideal. When job satisfaction is high, the discrepancy between existing perceptions and the ideal perceptions is small. As you complete Exercise 7, think about the conditions that replenish and invigorate you in your work as well as the issues and problems that seem to sap you of your focus and vitality. How does your current work setting match your ideal? What are your sources of satisfaction and frustration?

If you could design your ideal job, how close would your present position resemble your ideal job with respect to the following points:

	Not like my ideal at all		Somewhat resembles my ideal		Is my ideal
	1	**2**	**3**	**4**	**5**
Relationship with coworkers	_____	_____	_____	_____	_____
Relationship with supervisor	_____	_____	_____	_____	_____
The work itself	_____	_____	_____	_____	_____
Working conditions	_____	_____	_____	_____	_____
Pay and promotion opportunities	_____	_____	_____	_____	_____

Circle the three words below that best describe your current job:

challenging	exciting	oppressive
creative	fast-paced	relaxed
dead-end	fulfilling	rewarding
demanding	fun	stimulating
difficult	gratifying	stressful
draining	hectic	tedious
energizing	meaningful	unpredictable

What are the two most satisfying things about your job? What are the two most frustrating things about your job?

Satisfactions   **Frustrations**

1. _____   1. _____

2. _____   2. _____

In my research, I've found that sources of frustration for directors can be grouped into several categories: inability to achieve their professional goals; sacrifices in their personal life; salary that doesn't reflect the importance and demands of the job; the politics of dealing with various constituencies; the tendency for nitty-gritty managerial issues to eclipse leadership functions; and the director's perception of not being valued and supported by parents and teachers.

The irony from a mental health perspective is that many directors are clear about the constraints they face in achieving fulfillment but feel helpless in knowing how to modify their jobs to remedy the situation. This is unfortunate. The frustrations that directors experience are not inconsequential. The association between feeling a lack of accomplishment and burnout has been well demonstrated.

A Closer Look at Job Stress

Let's take a detour for a few minutes and explore this elusive concept we know as job stress. To be sure, research into the psychological characteristics of job stress is an imprecise science. The point at which daily frustrations can legitimately be classified as job stress is far from clear. But it is clear that stress and tension are part of the everyday lives of directors. Early childhood directors, like their principal counterparts at the elementary school level, lead hectic lives. Even the most-organized director is bombarded daily with frequent interruptions and petty annoyances. Although the amount of stress generated by the events of the day varies with the individual, stress is a constant in the lives of professionals in early childhood administrative positions.

The increasingly complex nature of the early childhood administrator's role is clearly impacting directors in adverse ways. For example, the rise in child-abuse allegations, the concern about infectious disease (including the transmission of AIDS), and the increased emphasis on participative management necessitates a different mind-set in directors' approaches to their job. This means that the daily concerns swimming in a director's head have changed.

In some centers, no longer are male caregivers allowed to supervise children alone; no longer is a simple bite by a rambunctious toddler considered a minor infraction; and no longer is decision making as quick and expedient as it once seemed. And today we have an ominous new stressor to contend with in our jobs as educators—the threat of terrorism and the psychological impact of fear on the children, their parents, and ourselves.

It is important that job stress not be viewed as a global construct, though. There are many different aspects of job stress that relate to the role of director. These include role conflict, role-personality conflict, role overload, role ambiguity, and role competence.

Be not afraid of growing slowly; be afraid only of standing still.

Chinese proverb

Role conflict. Role conflict is the occurrence of conflicting expectations whereby compliance with one makes it difficult to accommodate the other. These conflicting expectations may be due to differences in organizational demands and a director's own values, problems of resource allocation, or trying to accommodate the differing needs of so many people. Listen to the voices of Maria and Charmaine:

> *I don't know if I can handle it any longer. The corporate office wants me to increase the enrollments in every class. If I follow their dictate, I'll be out of compliance with licensing if all the children show up. Their prime concern is profit. I know that is important, but my prime concern is meeting the needs of the children by providing a quality program.*

> *How can I make the teachers understand? I would like to pay them more, I really would. But there is no way I can raise the tuition rates and make parents pay more. We don't get a subsidy like a lot of other programs. What I charge parents is all I have to work with. If I raise my rates too high in order to raise the teachers' salaries, I'll lose enrollments. It's simply a no-win situation!*

Role-personality conflict. Job stress can occur when there is a discrepancy between the expectations of a director's role and the needs and disposition of the person holding that role. In other words, certain kinds of jobs require certain personality dispositions. Most would agree, for example, that administering an early childhood program is sometimes, even often, a serendipitous enterprise— things seldom go as anticipated. There is an element of surprise every day on the job. If a director has a disposition of inflexibility and is not able to be spontaneous in responding to situations in new ways, role stress will surely occur. Jennifer reflects this tension:

> *I thought I would die. I had everything ready for our accreditation visit on Thursday. Wednesday afternoon we discovered we had a case of head lice. We had to completely sanitize all the housekeeping props and send home a letter to the parents informing them of the outbreak. My ulcer flared up. I was a nervous wreck by the time the assessor showed up on our doorstep the next morning. I'm thinking the stress just isn't worth it.*

When Jennifer completed Exercise 6, her idealized metaphor for the director's role was "a captain of an ocean liner, charting the course and providing a sense direction for all on board." The metaphor she used to describe her job, however, was "crashing down the white water, trying to navigate the rapids and stay on a raft." Through a series of reflective exercises similar to those you are doing in this book, Jennifer realized that she had been encouraged to take on the director's position even though her real love and passion was working directly with children in the classroom. This insight gave her the confidence to ask her board to hire a new director so she could return to the classroom as a lead teacher, a role more compatible with her personality and disposition.

Role overload. Role overload is when an individual simply doesn't have enough time or energy to do all that is expected of the job. Virtually all directors note this as being an issue with which they struggle. Whether role overload is due to the inability of a director to delegate, the lack of coordinating systems to handle everyday matters, or the unrealistic expectations for perfection that press upon some individuals, the outcome is the same—elevated feelings of inadequacy.

Unlike producing or selling a product, individuals working in the helping professions cannot quantify what they've achieved. Without clear indicators for measuring success, they often dwell on all that hasn't been accomplished in the course of a day. This can accentuate feelings of role overload. As LaToya states,

> I've been spinning all day—a hundred different interactions with children, teachers, and parents. Yet, here it is, 5:30, and I don't feel like I've accomplished anything. I know what I am doing is important, but I always have this nagging feeling there is so much more that I should be doing.

Role ambiguity. This type of job stress is simply the lack of information necessary to fulfill the obligations of the position. Role ambiguity relates to the clarity one has about job expectations. Both the quantity and the quality of information a director receives may be insufficient or too inconsistent to perform the job well. Directors may be unclear about what their coworkers expect of them or how their board or the owner of the center evaluates their performance. Dwaine says,

> I just don't get it. One week the owner wants me to be tough and penalize teachers for coming in late or being lax in their responsibilities. The next minute she tells me that they are underpaid and underappreciated so I should accommodate their individual needs. I'm frankly confused about what she expects of me.

Role competence. Role competence is a particular form of job stress in which a director acknowledges the lack of sufficient training, experience, and expertise to meet the demands of the job. Most common in novice directors, this type of job stress has individuals questioning their decision to become a director in the first place. The literature in this area refers to this phenomenon as the *imposter syndrome*. Roberta speaks to this experience:

I felt like such a fraud my first year on the job. If my board knew how incompetent I felt, they would have taken away my key to the front door. I can't believe they hired me, given my lack of qualifications and experience. They must have been really desperate or I must have been really convincing during my interview.

The evocative images that directors use to capture the essence of their administrative experience and the stories they share paint a portrait of real people in real situations, struggling with real problems. They also provide a glimpse into the future—the possibilities for reshaping roles, solving problems, and redirecting energies to achieve greater personal and professional fulfillment.

In his book *Mindfulness and Meaningful Work*, Claude Whitmyer stresses the importance of finding meaningful work and the Buddhist tradition of "right livelihood." He believes that work is no less necessary for our emotional and physical health than food or shelter. A fulfilling job has balance and diversity; it stretches and challenges; it taps our internal resources. It is the result of intention, not happenstance. Dissecting the elements of a job that support fulfillment is the starting point in this process. The goal is professional vitality—the ability to consistently work with passion and a strong inner sense of purpose.

I slept and dreamt that life was joy. I awoke and found that life was duty. I went to work, and discovered that duty can be joy.

Tagore, Bengali poet

CHAPTER 6

What's Your Style?

Day in and day out each of us makes important choices about how we define and present ourselves to the world. These preferences, like our fingerprints, are unique—they reflect our individual style, our personality. Understanding our preferences for the way we interact with people, process information, and go about our daily routines is central to achieving deeper insights and self-awareness.

To be sure, much of what we refer to as style is a set of automatic reflexes that we have learned through the years. Becoming more conscious of the nuances of our style and the effect of our style in different situations is important for two reasons. First, sometimes our perceptions of our style differ from others' perceptions. Recognizing this discrepancy is essential for ensuring successful interpersonal relations. Second, when we interact with people in a certain way, they are apt to respond to us in a certain way. As Rhonda Byrne, in her bestseller *The Secret*, explains, one of the operating principles of the universe is the law of attraction—what we put out is what we get back. If we are pessimistic about life, always viewing the glass as half empty, we will attract individuals who reinforce our world view. If we are optimistic, viewing the potential good in any situation, we will attract people with positive energy and circumstances who reinforce that world view.

Style has everything to do with the labels we give ourselves—organized or messy, risk taker or risk adverse, creative or not-so-creative, outgoing or withdrawn. It is not that labels are bad, it is just that labels can become a self-fulfilling prophesy. Individuals who are successful are more readily able to flex their style as needed. They are tuned in to the context of each new situation and the dynamics of the people involved and can adapt and adjust their style to be more effective.

There is certainly no shortage of tools available to assess different aspects of personality. In this chapter, you'll have a chance to focus on five aspects—your communication style, psychological type, learning style, preferred perceptual modality, and explanatory style. Caveat: These are not in-depth psychological assessments. Even so, they should serve as a springboard for thinking about your unique style and how you might flex that style to achieve the life you want.

Communication Style

No doubt about it, working in early childhood is intense. Every day you have hundreds of interactions with children, parents, and coworkers. Opportunities for being misunderstood are plentiful. Effective interpersonal relationships are the glue that holds early childhood programs together. An understanding of your communication style can give you a greater appreciation of the nuances that shape the way your messages are sent, received, and interpreted.

Appendix B,"Communication Style Audit," is a quick, easy-to-use assessment to promote greater self-awareness of your own communication style and greater sensitivity to the communication styles of others. This assessment draws on the seminal work of David Merrill, relating to personal style, and on Eileen Russo's application of Merrill's work to the area of communication. Russo conceptualizes communication style along two dimensions—assertiveness and expressiveness.

The dimension of assertiveness is the effort that a person makes to control the thoughts or actions of others. Assertive communicators tend to be direct, task oriented, and confident. Nonassertive communicators defer; they are more reserved, deliberate, and easygoing. The dimension of expressiveness describes the degree to which people exhibit or control their emotions and feelings while communicating. People who are expressive tend to show more vocal variation in their speech patterns and are more outgoing and demonstrative when talking. The intersection of these two dimensions results in four communication styles: direct, spirited, considerate, and systematic.

Direct. Direct communicators tell it like it is. They are decisive, take-charge people who like to be in control. They possess strong leadership skills, have the ability to get things done, and work single-mindedly toward their goals. Sometimes direct communicators can be perceived as being strong willed and overbearing. In their quest to get things done quickly, they may overlook important details. Focusing on others' feelings is not generally a strength of direct communicators, so they may be viewed in some interactions as lacking empathy.

Spirited. Spirited communicators are enthusiastic, friendly, and optimistic. They love to be around other people and enjoy the spotlight. They are good at building alliances and are able to motivate others and generate excitement about issues and projects. They enjoy a fast pace and are decisive. Spirited communicators are not always the best listeners. They can also exaggerate to make their point, behave impulsively, and gloss over important issues in an effort to rally support for their cause.

Considerate. People with a considerate communication style value warm, personal relationships with others. They are good listeners, reliable and steady, and supportive of others in a group. Because considerate communicators are easygoing, they may be reluctant to change, preferring to stick with what is comfortable. And because they want to avoid conflict, they may keep their opinions to themselves, give in too easily, and not achieve what they want to.

Systematic. People with a systematic communication style value accuracy and objectivity. They are analytical in their approach to problem solving and base their decision making on facts and data. They are persistent, orderly, and organized in their approach to their work and their relations with others. But systematic communicators can also be viewed as impersonal and detached, putting accuracy and detail ahead of other's feelings.

Take a moment now to reflect on your communication style. What do you consider to be the most positive aspects of your style? Think of some examples of how these positive aspects have benefited you in your personal and professional relationships. What are some aspects of your communication style that have hindered your effectiveness in interpersonal relationships? What do you think you can do to reduce or eliminate these hindrances?

Psychological Type

People differ in fundamental ways; they have distinct preferences for how they take in information and reach conclusions about the world. These different preferences for how we function are important because they govern both behavior (how we act in different situations) and beliefs (how we feel about different situations). A theory to explain these personality differences was first proposed by Carl Jung in 1923. Jung believed the similarities and differences in personality are not random but rather predictable.

In studying patterns of human behavior, particularly the way people perceive information and interpret reality, Jung concluded that people are born with a predisposition for certain preferences. In Jungian theory, behavior relates to basic functions involved in gathering information about one's world and making decisions based on that information. Jung's theory was popularized by Katherine Briggs and Isabel Briggs Myers, who developed the Myers-Briggs Type Indicator (MBTI). The work of Jung and Myers is important because an understanding of the different psychological types can elicit a deeper appreciation for those who function differently from us.

The following is a brief introduction to the concept and terminology of psychological type. If you are interested in determining your precise typology, I encourage you to contact a psychologist or counselor who is professionally qualified to administer the MBTI. In my book *Blueprint for Action*, I have included an assessment of psychological type that you can also use for this purpose. Additionally, there are several sites on the Internet that provide this service.

Extraversion/Introversion. The extraversion/introversion dimension has to do with the source, direction, and focus of one's energy. Extraverts are energized by the outer world. They are actively involved with people and things around them. For introverts, reflection, introspection, and solitude produce energy, focus, and attention. Introverts are more involved with concepts and ideas. They turn to the inner world of ideas and private thoughts.

Sensing/Intuition. The sensing/intuition dimension has to do with how we gather information and perceive reality. Sensing types look at facts and details. They tend to be down-to-earth, literal, and realistic. Sensing types are sequential in their thinking and rely on their five senses as a means of gathering information. They prefer the practical and enjoy hands-on, tangible experiences. Intuition types, on the other hand, are concerned with the big picture, the grand scheme of things. They are more abstract in the way they process information. Intuition types tend to look at the relationships between things. They strive to understand the meaning of situations in order to achieve insight and solve problems.

Thinking/Feeling. The thinking/feeling dimension relates to how we make decisions about the information we've gathered. Thinking types tend to be very objective and analytical. They are logical in their decision-making processes and purposefully impersonal. Thinking types weigh facts objectively, considering all sides of an issue, including the consequences of a decision. Feeling types are more subjective, using their personal value system for making decisions. Understanding people, achieving harmony, and feeling compassion are important to feeling types. They tend to need approval and personal support more than they need to succeed in intellectual tasks. Don't let the labels for this dimension mislead you. Thinking types certainly have feelings and feeling types surely have the capacity to think. When making decisions, however, their modes for arriving at a decision are very different.

Judging/Perceiving. The final dimension, judging/perceiving, has to do with how we structure our lives—our lifestyle orientation. Judging types tend to have rather structured, scheduled, and organized personal and professional lives. They are decisive and deliberate when making decisions; they see a right way to do things and proceed accordingly. Perceiving types, on the other hand, need variety, novelty, and change. They prefer to stand back and use a wait-and-see style when confronted with the need to make a decision. They often have a poor concept of time and feel comfortable with a go-with-the-flow attitude toward life. They are more flexible, spontaneous, and adaptable than judging types.

Learning Style

The term *learning style* describes the multiple ways people make sense of their world. It includes the diverse ways we decode, encode, process, store, and retrieve information as well as the emotional and environmental elements that affect motivation and desire to learn. A person's learning style clearly influences his or her receptivity to different instructional strategies and the degree to which concepts are internalized. Understanding differences in learning style can help us understand why some learning experiences may be stimulating and interesting to some people while downright boring to others.

Although each person's learning style is shaped by biology, it is also modified by experience. Learning style influences preference for learning activities and situations. Some people learn best by reflecting, others learn by observing, and still others acquire new skills best by doing. While some people relish the idea of using a group setting to discuss problems and situations at length, others see this approach as time consuming and cumbersome.

The work of Anthony Gregorc provides a useful framework for thinking about different learning styles. He proposed that there are two ways individuals perceive information—concretely and abstractly—and two ways they process and organize information—sequentially and randomly. Although everyone uses all these perceptual and processing modes to some degree, the unique combination of where people fall on these two intersecting continua create unique learning styles.

Drawing on the conceptual framework from Gregorc, Appendix C, "Learning Style Inventory," will help you determine your preferred learning style. Remember as you complete this assessment that there are no right or wrong answers. A description of each style follows.

Practical learners (concrete-sequential). More than anything else, practical learners want to see the real-life application of the ideas they are learning. Their favorite question is, "How can I use this?" They learn through direct experience and want tangible evidence of learning in the form of handouts, products, notes, and recipes. In meetings, it is important for practical learners to have a sense of where the discussion is heading and what is going to be accomplished, so a detailed agenda is essential. In workshops, they get impatient when other participants ramble or stray from the point. They are interested in facts and details, so step-by-step directions are important.

Analytic learners (abstract-sequential). Analytic learners weigh the pros and cons, advantages and disadvantages, and good and bad of each issue presented in different learning experiences. They tend to be verbal—the ones tossing out the hard questions and challenging instructors for their rationale, the logic, or the research backing their statements. Their favorite question is, "How do you know this is true?" They live in the world of abstract ideas, see the big picture, and enjoy analyzing every angle of a situation. They use facts to prove or disprove theories. Analytic learners are quite content to sit through lectures and can become impatient with cooperative learning strategies or activities in which participants process information in small groups.

Imaginative learners (abstract-random). Imaginative learners are people-people. They focus on the processes of learning more than the content. For them, learning must be personalized; their emotions influence their ability to concentrate. Imaginative learners thrive on personal meaning and personal involvement in any learning situation. Their favorite question is, "Why is this important?" Small-group discussions and in-depth sharing with a learning partner are favorite instructional strategies with these individuals. Imaginative learners need a lot of time to reflect and process ideas. They often engage in flights of fantasy, sprinkle their conversation with superlatives, and focus on the big picture at the risk of missing the details.

Inventive learners (concrete-random). Inventive learners need a lot of mental elbowroom. They use experimentation as well as insight and instinct to solve problems. Inventive learners make intuitive leaps and take risks to come up with novel ways to solve problems. They may test poorly because they think too much about the nuances of questions. Inventive learners need flexibility in instructional strategies so they can create innovative spin-offs. Their favorite question is, "What if ...?" While inventive learners think on their feet and are inquisitive and independent, they can also be impulsive.

Learning theorists Rita and Kenneth Dunn remind us that learning style is more than just our preference for how we perceive and process information. To fully understand the multiple ways that people learn, they believe it is also important to consider the environmental, emotional, sociological, and physical aspects that promote learning. Here are some questions to get you thinking about these other dimensions of your learning style.

Environmental elements

- **Sound:** Do you learn best with music playing in the background, or do you need absolute quiet to concentrate? Are you able to screen out people's conversations and other extraneous environmental noise when you read or concentrate on a task?

- **Light.** Do you find either bright or dim lights distracting? Do you work best in natural, filtered daylight?

- **Temperature.** Are you affected by extremes in ambient temperature? Do you prefer cool, warm, or moderate temperatures in which to learn?

- **Design.** When you read something that requires your full attention, do you prefer to sit in an easy chair or a straight-back chair, or do you like to stretch out on the floor? Do you prefer a formal or informal room arrangement when you attend a workshop or lecture?

Emotional elements

- **Motivation.** Under what learning conditions do your sources of motivation differ? When do you need extrinsic reinforcement (praise, grades, pay) to encourage you to tackle new knowledge and skill areas? Under what conditions are you intrinsically motivated to learn something new?

- **Persistence.** How would you describe yourself with respect to your level of persistence in learning new things? Do you prefer to set short, achievable goals, or do you have a level of persistence that allows you to tackle long-range goals?

- **Responsibility.** Under what conditions are you most likely to take responsibility for your own learning?

- **Structure.** Do you like to have new areas of learning highly structured and tightly supervised, or do you prefer to set your own goals and monitor your own progress?

Sociological elements

- **Grouping.** Which types of things do you learn best on your own, in small groups, or in large groups? What kinds of collegial staff development experiences do you find most rewarding?

Physical elements

- **Intake.** How important is it to you to have something to eat or nibble on when you focus on a new task? Do you like to chew gum or drink something while you master something new?

- **Time.** Some people are more alert in the morning; others prefer to tackle new learning tasks in the afternoon or evening. What is your preference?

- **Mobility.** When you attend a staff development workshop, do you need to get up and move around at regular intervals? When you work at a computer or when you read, do you like to take frequent breaks to stretch your muscles, or can you sit and concentrate for long periods?

Preferred Perceptual Modality

Another way to conceptualize style is to think about your preferred perceptual modality. Some people are *visual* learners and benefit from detailed flipcharts, overhead transparencies, and handouts. Others are mainly *auditory*, preferring lecture, debate, and group discussions. And still others have a *kinesthetic* modality preference, preferring to learn new things by moving, touching, and engaging in action-oriented activities.

We are what we repeatedly do. Excellence, then, is not an act, but a habit.

Aristotle

Adapted from the work of Barbe and Swassing, Appendix D, "Preferred Perceptual Modality," provides a brief assessment that will help you understand your perceptual preferences. The following is a description of each modality:

Visual learners. Visual learners learn best when information is written out. They prefer diagrams, charts, and tables as learning aids and enjoy media such as films, videos, and pictures. They are the coworkers who always comment on the outfit you are wearing or the earrings you have chosen as an accessory. When given a choice of where to sit at a meeting or workshop, they'll choose the front of the room so they can easily see the presenter and the visuals being used.

Visual learners like working in an office or classroom that is aesthetically pleasing, not too distracting or cluttered. They appreciate handouts and will notice details like a misspelled word on a transparency. Visual learners often have trouble remembering verbal instructions and would rather read than be read to. They like to take notes or doodle during meetings or workshops, although there is no guarantee they will refer to these notes once they leave the session.

Auditory learners. Auditory learners learn best by hearing things spoken. They prefer small- and large-group discussions, lectures, storytelling, and audiotapes as instructional aids. Auditory learners appreciate good speakers. They are able to recall the specifics of what was said as well as how it was said.

Auditory learners often have an inner dialogue going on during a meeting or presentation and play with the pros and cons of an issue to clarify concepts internally. They are generally talkative and love discussions, but they can get carried away with lengthy descriptions.

Kinesthetic learners. Learners with this perceptual modality style learn best by touching, moving, and feeling. Kinesthetic learners like to be actively involved in learning new things. They learn best by manipulating objects, acting out scenarios, and playing games. When given a choice, kinesthetic learners sit at the rear of a meeting or workshop room so they can stretch out, move around, or get up and go to the restroom when necessary.

Kinesthetic learners use action words and gestures when speaking. They enjoy role-playing, dramatizations, games, and any type of activity where they are physically engaged in the learning process. Kinesthetic learners tend to gesture more than visual or auditory learners. They may touch another person to get their attention and use a finger to guide their reading. Variety and action are crucial for kinesthetic learners. They can't sit for long periods of time.

Explanatory Style

Our explanatory style is how we explain the events—good or bad—that we experience. For most people this is not something they are consciously aware of; it is the internal dialogues or thought processes that occur throughout daily activities. Martin Seligman, a pioneer in this area of research, says that when faced with positive or challenging events in life, a person's explanatory style determines whether they view the world through an *optimistic* or *pessimistic* lens.

Take a minute to read these two scenarios describing a negative and positive event:

- You apply for a promotion for a higher-level position in your child care agency. You are among three candidates interviewed by the executive director. You learn a few days later that one of the other candidates has been offered the position.

- You have never made a workshop presentation at your state early childhood conference before. You submit a proposal and it is accepted.

Now these exact scenarios may not have happened to you, but as you read the three Ps that make up your explanatory style—*personalization, permanence*, and *pervasiveness*—think about how you have reacted in the past to negative and positive events. Do you identify with the optimist or the pessimist?

Personalization. Personalization addresses the question, *Who caused the situation?* In the first scenario, a pessimist will blame herself. "I'm lousy at interviews; no wonder I didn't get the job." An optimist, in contrast, will not blame herself, but will consider other factors. "Someone else was more experienced and a better fit for the position." She will not take the rejection personally. In the second scenario, a pessimist may think, "Wow, the selection committee must not have had very many proposals." In contrast the optimist will conclude that she deserved to be selected: "I submitted a great proposal; that is why I was selected."

In general, pessimists internalize blame for the negative events that occur in their lives and attribute positive events to something external. Optimists, on the other hand, take credit for the positive events in their lives and attribute negative events to something external.

Permanence. Permanence addresses the question, *How long will the situation last?* In the first scenario, the pessimist may think, "What's the use of trying. I'll never get a promotion here." Meanwhile the optimist will conclude, "Even though it didn't work out this time, I'll apply again the next time an opening occurs." In the positive scenario, the pessimist may think, "Wow, the stars were lined up right. I was really lucky to be selected. Probably never happen again." The optimist will think, "I've got a new way to share my talents. I'll submit a proposal next year, too."

In general, pessimists think that negative events are likely to repeat themselves. They'll say, "I'll never get a promotion," "I'll never get married," "I'll never loose these last 25 pounds." Optimists view negative events as isolated and anticipate that things will be better tomorrow.

Pervasiveness. Pervasiveness addresses the question, *How does this event impact my life situation?* In the negative scenario, the pessimist may think, "Guess they've made it clear to me; I haven't got what it takes to handle a leadership position. I better not think about running for president of my condo association either." The optimist, on the other hand, will treat the negative event as contained to the specific situation, "If I can't advance in this agency, I'll seek out other options elsewhere to hone my leadership skills."

In the positive scenario, the situation is reversed. The pessimist interprets her selection as a presenter as an isolated event: "I better not get cocky. Just because my proposal was accepted for this conference doesn't mean I'll be accepted at the regional conference." The optimist, on the other hand, will not interpret the positive event as restricted to this one sphere: "If my proposal was good enough to be accepted, then maybe I should also try submitting an article for publication in the AEYC state newsletter."

In general, pessimists view negative events as spilling over into other areas of their life. Optimists, on the other hand, view negative events more narrowly, limited to that specific situation. Pessimists view positive events as confined to the specific situation, whereas optimists may extrapolate a positive event to other areas of their life.

Explanatory style is complex. People can be pessimistic in some areas of their life but optimistic in others. In general, though, most people tend to think optimistically or pessimistically about the things that happen to them. These differing explanations have profound implications for you as an early childhood administrator. Your explanatory style impacts how you handle adversity, the attitude you convey to your staff and parents, and the overall climate of your program.

So what was the greatest work-related challenge you faced this past week? What was the most positive event you experienced this past week? Which explanatory style characterized your responses to these events?

No pessimist ever discovered the secrets of the stars, or sailed to an uncharted land, or opened a new heaven to the human spirit.

Helen Keller

CHAPTER 7

Avoiding Burnout

Being an administrator of an early childhood program is not just a state of employment; it is a state of mind. So many individuals who don the director's hat with noble intentions of creating exemplary centers end up leaving the field frustrated, depleted, and disillusioned. They simply burn out. When the joy of interacting with children, teachers, and parents slips away, disillusionment with the job settles in and manifests itself in a growing cynicism, a smothering of the spirit.

People don't burn out because they work too hard, but rather from a sense of futility, the belief that all their hard work isn't making a difference. Unlike the muscular exhaustion that results from playing three sets of tennis or running a race, individuals experiencing burnout describe their exhaustion as being a total fatigue from which they can't seem to spring back. In their metaphors they describe their feelings of energy depletion. One director used the visual image of limp spaghetti, another wilted flowers, and still another described her state as a well run dry. The most poignant of all was a director who confided, "I feel like I am slowly suffocating, like I'm sinking in quicksand."

Are you a candidate for burnout? Take a minute to complete Exercise 8 and reflect on the level of stress you experience in your own job.

exercise 8

	Seldom	Sometimes	Often
Do you lose sleep worrying about your job?	____	____	____
Do you dread leaving your center for a short vacation because of the mountain of work that will pile up in your absence?	____	____	____
Do you feel emotionally drained from your work?	____	____	____
Do you feel like you are always "putting out fires" and lack time to do the planning that will help prevent crises?	____	____	____

	Seldom	Sometimes	Often

Do you feel you do the work of several people and handle many things not in line with your job description? _____ _____ _____

Do you feel others don't appreciate how hard you work? _____ _____ _____

Do you feel isolated, with no one to consult or talk to about your job frustrations? _____ _____ _____

Do you feel overwhelmed by pending deadlines for proposals and reports that are due? _____ _____ _____

Do you find yourself apologizing for how long it takes you to return phone messages or answer e-mails? _____ _____ _____

Do you feel your job doesn't make good use of your talents and skills? _____ _____ _____

Does your work consume your whole life, rarely allowing time for you to pursue outside interests? _____ _____ _____

Do you worry excessively about pleasing others? _____ _____ _____

Are there things you'd like to do, but cannot because you're simply too tired, ill, or out of shape? _____ _____ _____

Do you ever contemplate quitting your job? _____ _____ _____

> *Maintaining a complicated life is a great way to avoid changing it.*
>
> *Elaine St. James*

So where do you stand on the continuum of emotional commitment to your job? If you answered *often* to more than half of these questions, you may be at risk for becoming another burnout statistic. The irony from a mental health perspective is that while many directors express concern that they cannot continue to perform their job at their current level of intensity, they feel helpless in knowing how to modify their jobs to be more manageable.

Not withstanding all the pressures inherent in their positions, many directors find their jobs stimulating, challenging, and personally rewarding. As you can imagine, the metaphors they use to describe their jobs are quite different. They are metaphors filled with hope and possibility—a flower bursting into bloom, climbing a mountain and taking in new vistas, watching a Polaroid picture emerge.

These directors have developed a repertoire of skills and personal strategies as well as the mental attitude that allows them to grow, indeed thrive, in their roles. I use the word *thrive* purposefully. Some people talk about coping with stress, but to me coping implies you're hanging on by a thread. Why not strive for something higher—creating a job suffused with excitement, engagement, passion, challenge, creativity, and joy.

This chapter draws on the collective wisdom of the thrivers in our field. The strategies you'll read about are probably not new to you. The key is that individuals in control of their personal and professional lives have a deliberate game plan. They are well informed, sensitive to the stress indicators in their lives, and realistic in assessing their skills and resources. They have learned to put their jobs in perspective by adding diversity and interest to their lives. They know how to use their time wisely, and they believe in the value of self-talk to help them stay focused. In other words, people who thrive in early childhood education do not do so by happenstance. Their actions declare that they are not passive about their destiny, not controlled by events. Rather, they are active in shaping their lives, day by day.

Tuning in to the Stressors in Your Life

Stress is a complex phenomenon because there is no single identifiable profile or set of reactions that apply to all people. Stress covers a wide range of physical, behavioral, and psychological symptoms. Physical symptoms may include a headache, backache, a stiff neck, an upset stomach, a tight feeling across the chest. Psychological symptoms include all those feelings associated with stressful situations—feeling overwhelmed or inadequate, feeling guilty or anxious, or just plain worrying. Behavioral symptoms are the things people do when they are under stress—yell, sulk, eat, bite their nails, smoke, or drink.

The key is to become aware of the stress indicators in your own life. Listen to your body. Tune in to the inner tension, aches, and subtle changes in your energy level. What drains you? For each individual these symptoms will be different. Sensitizers are keenly aware when their body is experiencing stress. Repressors, on the other hand, ignore the signs or try to counter negative symptoms by pushing harder and working longer.

If someone throws you a ball, you don't have to catch it.

Richard Carlson

65

"I think I'm feeling stressed!"

Being a sensitizer also means being aware of the internal sources of stress that may affect your personal and professional fulfillment. These sources may be related to dispositions such as being inflexible, being excessively competitive, or being a perfectionist. They might also be related to a host of irrational beliefs that can build anxiety:

- You must be loved (or at least liked) by everyone

- You must be competent in everything you do

- Unhappiness is caused by external events

- There is a perfect solution to everything

- There is a perfect relationship waiting to be discovered

- Things are, or ought to be, fair and just

- If you don't please others, they will abandon you

- Conflict is bad and undesirable

- Mistakes are a source of shame

- The past determines the present

- Your worth as an individual depends on how much you achieve

The important point is that every person has a different profile: one person's stress is another's stimulant for peak performance. Hans Selye, a pioneer in the area of stress research, reminds us that it is our ability to cope with the demands in our personal and professional lives that counts, not the quality or intensity of those demands. Both good events (buying a new house, the birth of a baby, winning the lottery) and negative events (an argument with your partner, a traffic ticket, a lost wallet) can cause stress and produce the same biochemical reaction in your body.

Perhaps a more concrete way to conceptualize stress is to think of the notion of *load* and *overload*. At some point in your life you've probably been in an elevator that exceeded the recommended load capacity posted on the framed certificate of operation. An alarm might have gone off or the elevator doors wouldn't shut. Like an elevator, each of us has a maximum load capacity that dictates the physical, emotional, and mental demands our body can endure before it simply shuts down.

Our physical limits are easy to grasp. We might be able to carry 10 bags of groceries from our car to our kitchen, no sweat. But if we had to carry 100 bags those 20 yards, we'd surely feel the strain in our muscles and joints. Emotional limits are a bit trickier to recognize. We might be able to handle an angry employee, the death of a beloved pet, and an overdrawn check on the same day and still keep our cool, but if we got rear-ended by another car on the way home from work, we'd probably lose our composure. Mentally, too, we have limits. When we're given too much information to absorb in too short a time, our brain short-circuits. Our short-term memory falters, and we may fumble for words when trying to talk.

As Richard Swensen points out in his book *The Overload Syndrome*, the tendency in our culture is to keep adding more to our lives: one more option, one more commitment, one more expectation, one more purchase, one more debt, one more change, one more job, and one more decision. People today deal with more "things per person" than at any other time in history. The threshold point where breakdown begins obviously varies from person to person. The key is to be acutely aware of your own physical, emotional, and mental load capacity and be able to adjust as needed so you don't exceed your threshold.

Striving for Balance

I don't believe we do an adequate job in our field of training early childhood educators how to compartmentalize, to define the emotional limits of their work, and how to mentally close the door at the end of a day's work. Psychologists use the term *affective neutrality* to describe the capacity to balance compassion with emotional detachment. This is an essential skill for becoming a long-term thriver in the early childhood field. The situation is made more difficult by the fact that so many directors are also mothers who leave their full-time jobs to go home to another full-time job of caretaking.

The trouble with the rat race is that even if you win, you're still the rat!

Lily Tomlin

Achieving a balance also means diversifying your interests. Well-rounded people don't define who they are solely by their professional accomplishments. What we do in our leisure time is as essential to our success as what we do during our working hours. Hillary Rodham Clinton had it right when she said, "Don't confuse having a career with having a life. They are not the same thing." Hans Selye made the same point when he said, "The human body, like tires of a car, wears longest when it wears evenly."

So what does balance mean for you as you think about your personal and professional identities? How do you define balance in terms of giving and receiving, talking and listening, planning and acting spontaneously, being alone and being together, the present and the future, variety and routine, seriousness and silliness, and all the other yin and yang tensions that make up a vibrant life?

Embracing a New Mantra: "Simplicity Is Power"

In his provocative book *The Paradox of Choice*, Barry Schwartz makes the counterintuitive case that eliminating choice can greatly reduce the stress, anxiety, and busyness of our lives. He argues that the world today offers us more choices but, ironically, less satisfaction. Whether we're buying jeans at the GAP, deciding which coffee combo to purchase at Starbucks, or which station to watch on our 100+ channel cable network, everyday decisions from the mundane to the weighty have become increasingly complex. Most people assume that more choice means better options and greater satisfaction, but in reality choice overload sets us up for unrealistically high expectations and more stress. The fact that some choice is good doesn't necessarily mean that more choice is better.

The simplicity movement is challenging the notion that more is better not only in terms of the choices we have, but also in terms of the possessions we accumulate, the activities we take part in, the commitments we make, and the information we have access to. Simplicity is the art of doing less of what doesn't matter and focusing more on what does matter. While many people long for simplicity, thrivers take conscious steps in their lives to make it happen. Their motto is, *The secret to happiness lies not in getting more, but in wanting less.*

Consciously think of ways you can streamline your life. At work strive for substance over bureaucracy. Keep memos short, policies crisp, and words to a minimum. Go for the essence. Look for ways to streamline your program's operations without compromising quality. At home, don't allow things to accumulate that no longer have a real function. "If you get rid of it, you don't have to organize it," says Elaine St. James, author of the bestseller *Simplify Your Life*.

The road to simplicity is made up of small steps. Take a hard look at the influence of television in your life. Do the lives portrayed on your favorite shows contribute anything positive to your life? Consciously filter the thousands of advertising messages you take in daily. Our consumer-driven society bombards us with advertising designed to make us perpetually dissatisfied. Counter with your own discerning criteria to distinguish needs from wants. See owning as a liability rather than an asset. Everything we own requires a commitment of our working time to earn money to pay for it and our leisure time to use and care for it. Accumulating things we don't need merely complicates life.

Environmental responsibility alone should keep us from buying the majority of the gadgets advertised today. Think *green*—seek ways you can help to preserve the delicate balance needed for our planet to survive. You've heard the statistics. The United States has less than 6% of the world's population, but consumes about 33% of the world's energy. I recently read that the energy used by air conditioners alone in the U.S. is equal to the amount of energy used by the entire country of China.

Adopting Wellness as a Lifestyle

No need to preach on this one; you've heard the message a thousand times. What we eat, how often and how vigorously we exercise, and the things we do to calm our body and mind have a decided impact on our well-being and longevity. While we can attribute our genetic predispositions to our parents, the truth is, the daily choices we make by and large determine how energized we feel, how robust our immune system is, and how we react to the stressors of modern life.

There is certainly no shortage of lifestyle experts to provide guidance on what to eat, how to exercise, and how to replenish our spirit. My favorites are Andrew Weil, Bob Green, Chris Crowley, and Michael Roizen. The expert or guru you follow is less important than the fact that you make wellness a high priority in your life. Yes, it takes time to become informed about health and nutrition. Yes, it's hard to kick bad habits like smoking and snacking on high-fat, high-calorie foods. And yes, it takes extraordinary effort to stick to a diet and a daily exercise regime. But in the end, we can't dispute the advice of Grace Mirabella, founder of *Mirabella Magazine*, who said, "The name of the game is taking care of yourself because you're going to live long enough to wish you had!"

All true leaders have learned to say no to the good in order to say yes to the best.

John Maxwell

Cherish your health: If it is good, preserve it. If it is unstable, improve it. If it is beyond what you can improve, get help.

George Carlin

If you are not convinced about the merits of adopting wellness as a lifestyle, then just think of it as part of your job description. As a leader in your organization, you are an influential role model for the staff, children, and parents of your program. The conscious decisions you make about your own healthful habits clearly impact the overall wellness of your program.

Adopting wellness as a lifestyle also means carving out time for some positive self-indulgence. Everyone needs and deserves time for renewing body and spirit. Those who have no fire inside themselves cannot warm others. The energy and commitment required to cultivate the mind and spirit are not easily mobilized after a long, hard day at work. That is why thrivers take deliberate steps to carve out time for creative and recuperative growth.

Become deliberate about your self-care. Managing personal time means consciously setting aside a portion of each day for pursuits that enrich your mind and replenish your spirit. William Glasser calls these commitments to self *positive addictions*. Ceramics, guitar, yoga, meditation, photography, jogging, or just soaking in a tub full of bubbles in a candlelit room—it doesn't matter what the indulgence is as long as you have something that makes you feel special.

If you are going to build immunity to burnout, it is important to adopt concrete strategies to calm the body and mind—not easy in a world where we measure daily tasks in nanoseconds, where we're irritated if someone doesn't answer the phone in two rings. In his book *The End of Patience*, David Shenk says quickness has disappeared from our culture. We now experience only degrees of slowness. With conveniences like FAX machines, e-mail, overnight delivery services, beepers, cell phones, and BlackBerrys, we've managed to compress time to such an extent that we are painfully aware of every second we wait for anything. Shenk believes this has made us more impatient with traffic, restaurant service, and elevators. The irony is that we seldom ask ourselves if anything is really being gained by speeding up everything. Years ago Mahatma Gandhi said, "There's more to life than just increasing its speed." That aphorism holds true today.

The problem with all this speed and the frantic energy spent keeping up, writes David Brooks in *Newsweek*, is that it undermines creativity: "Creativity is what happens when you're in the shower and your brain has time to noodle about and create the odd connections that lead to new ideas." If your brain is always multitasking, there is no time or energy for undirected mental play.

Thrivers have developed their own unique recipe for calming their body and their mind. Their strategies are as varied as the individuals I have interviewed who represent this group. For some thrivers, calmness is achieved through certain rituals—these are simple routines that celebrate special moments. One director I know gets up before the rest of the family so she can have her cup of coffee and eat her muffin while sitting on the back porch, watching the sunrise over the lake behind her house. For another, it is writing in a gratitude journal before bedtime, a special way to attain some reflective closure at the end of a busy day.

Cultivating a Strong Support Network

Every year *Working Mother* magazine summarizes the accomplishments of the 25 most influential working mothers in America. One recent honoree said, "I don't believe in juggling. What you have to do is create a life that is a web of work and home, community, family, friends, teachers, and neighbors. Webs are strong." Virtually all indicated that in their homes, they had abandoned traditional roles, instead looking at the total responsibilities of what needed to be done, distributing work among all family members.

In all occupations, the people who tend to cope best with stress have a network of family and friends to turn to for sympathy and support. Developing a support network, cultivating closeness, and maintaining close, trusting relationships serves as a safety valve. Whether they study people or rabbits, researchers find that intimacy promotes health while isolation fosters stress, disease, and early death. It seems there is some empirical support for the cliché, "Good friends are good medicine." Social isolation is statistically just as unhealthy as smoking, high blood pressure, high cholesterol, obesity, or lack of exercise. Finding a companion—any companion, from a fish to a significant other—can buffer us from stress.

There is another aspect to the social support that I have found in my research, and that is that thrivers try to surround themselves with people who lift their spirits, who make them smile and laugh. Yes, it's good to have friends, but it's even better to actively seek out friends who are optimistic about life.

Exercise 9 provides an opportunity for you to think about your immediate circle of friends, family, and colleagues. Who can you count on? Who elevates your spirits and energizes you? Who drains you and adds stress to your life? In whose presence do you find yourself being the best of who you are?

Add the names of your eight closest colleagues, family members, or friends to the circles that surround you. Draw lines connecting each person to you. Make a straight bold line (——————) if the source of that support is strong and vibrant. Make a broken line (- - - - - - -) if that support is unpredictable. Make a zigzag line (〰〰〰) if your relationship with that person creates tension and stress.

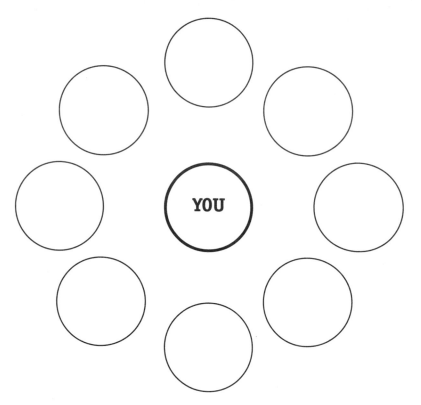

Now ask yourself the following questions:

- Can you be yourself with this person? Do you feel accepted and respected in all your interactions?

- Does your relationship with this person provide a balanced exchange of support?

- Does this person share your most cherished values? Do you talk about values together?

- Do you feel energized when you are around this person, or do your interactions drain you?

- Is this person genuinely concerned about your happiness? Are you able to genuinely celebrate his or her successes?

Managing Time from the Inside Out

Ever since man observed the first dawn, he has wrestled with the mysteries of time and the inexplicable nature of its daily cycles. Time is the raw material of life, weaving its way through every aspect of our existence. We talk about having "a great time" or the "time of our life." We can waste time, lose time, pass the time away, and even march to its rhythms, but we'll never be able to increase time or stop time.

In the past, status was marked by how much leisure time a person had. To be idle was to be a member of the privileged class. Now we measure status by how busy we are; how hard we work. Our high-velocity life in contemporary America demands greater speed, capacity, and capabilities. If we understand our time orientation, our sensitivity to time, and the influence of time on our own behavior, we can maximize its potential in our lives. Begin by asking yourself the following questions:

- What were the spoken or unspoken messages your parents taught you about time? What do you remember about how you viewed the passage of time during your childhood years?

- As an adult, what percentage of your time do you spend thinking about the past, the present, or the future?

- How is time related to the pleasurable and unpleasant moments in your life? When do you feel like time flies? When do you feel like the minutes drag on for eternity?

- How would you rate your sensitivity to time? Do you feel lost without your watch? Do you need an alarm clock to wake up in the morning? Do you get annoyed when someone shows up late to an appointment? Do you get impatient waiting in a line at the grocery store or caught in traffic?

- How do you handle time pressures? Do you get a surge of adrenaline when confronted with an impending deadline or do you get immobilized by the stress that the time-crunch creates?

- What behaviors are characteristic of how you manage your time? Do you regularly multitask, trying to do two or more things at once? Do you tend to underestimate how much time a particular project will take? How often do you procrastinate so that unpleasant tasks become panic situations?

- What are your general feelings associated with how you use your time? Do you feel you must always be busy doing something productive? Do you feel somewhat guilty if you relax?

Self care is never a selfish act—it is simply good stewardship of the only gift we have, the gift we were put on earth to offer to others.

Parker Palmer

- How would you characterize your general pace as it relates to time? Do you find yourself driving too fast, eating too fast, and in a constant battle with the clock?

- How do your biorhythms impact how you schedule your time? When during the day is your concentration level sharpest? When do you experience your peak energy level? During which part of the day are you apt to feel frustrated or pressured?

- How does your use of time impact the quality of your relationships? Are any of your primary relationships time starved? Do you feel you have a sufficient cushion of time in your life so you can respond to the unexpected needs of those you care most about?

In many ways the term *time management* is a misnomer. We can't really manage the clock. We can't accumulate time, save it, or store it, and once spent, we can't retrieve it. All we can do is manage ourselves so we use time more efficiently and effectively. The interesting thing about time is that it is equitably distributed to each of us. We all must live within the constraints of 168 hours a week, whether we are a captain of industry or a bus driver. So our problem is not a lack of time—we have all there is—but rather what we do with the time we have.

Managing time from the inside out means shifting our perspective from thinking about time as a convenient unit of measure to thinking about it as a qualitative reflection of the richness of our life. If we think about time as a mere unit of measure, we'll perpetuate the insanity of trying to squeeze more tasks, more interactions, and more projects into the 24 hours we're allotted each day. If we think about time as a qualitative reflection of the richness of our life, it forces us evaluate what we are doing in those precious hours. So here's the million-dollar question: Do the tasks, interactions, and projects that take up your time truly reflect your core values and highest priorities?

Learning the Value of Self-Talk

Over a century ago, William James wrote, "The greatest discovery of my generation is that a human being can alter his life by altering his attitudes of mind." How true those words still are today. We all know of people who are blessed with enormous privilege and squander their good fortune, while others who are presented with seemingly insurmountable hardships go on to achieve phenomenal success. The distinction, I believe, has everything to do with attitude.

It is true that stress is inherent in our culture. We can't stop traffic jams, terrorists, rising gas prices, and computers that crash, but we can learn to control our attitude toward the events we experience. Our attitude is directly related to our locus of control—the degree to which we feel in command of our own

Change your thoughts and you change your world.

Norman Vincent Peale

destiny. People with an internal locus of control are less anxious, more trusting, and willing to remedy their personal problems. People with an external locus of control feel like they are victims; they are quick to find fault with the world.

I heard recently that the average person has around fifty thousand thoughts each day. Some of these thoughts are positive; others are negative; the remaining are neutral. In a very real sense, we have only three options for how we deal with the portion of negative thoughts we process every day. We can choose to simply ignore them by clicking the mental mouse in our brain and sending them to the recycle bin. We can choose to dwell on them, even catastrophize them, and add them to the list of things causing us anxiety. Or we can choose to engage in self-talk in an effort to render them neutral or even recast them in positive terms. In other words, we have enormous power to control how we interpret everything that happens to us.

In his wonderful book *Falling Awake*, Dave Ellis says that the sum total of the words we use to describe any experience become our interpretation of that experience. If we say that we're exhausted when we're really just tired, we might feel more drained than we are. If we describe ourselves as terrified instead of just frightened, we probably increase our level of anxiety. In many cases, our happiness quotient has more to do with the way we interpret our circumstances then with the circumstances themselves. By learning to manage the way we interpret our experiences, we can alter our well-being.

This chapter was not intended to give you sweaty palms, a tense back, or blurred vision. Yes, burnout is a serious problem, but don't let your awareness of the issue render you immobile. The important point to remember is that you have enormous control over the factors that impact our personal and professional fulfillment. The key is to be able to recognize when your circuits register an overload, when your battery needs recharging, and when you've simply got too much spam cluttering your life. *Dedication does not have to mean deadication.*

When we truly care for ourselves, it becomes possible to care more profoundly for other people. The more alert and sensitive we are to our own needs, the more loving and generous we can be toward others

Eda LeShan

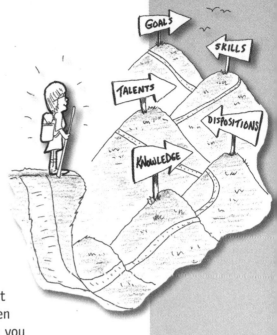

CHAPTER 8

The Next Step—Mapping Your Journey

So what are you doing for the rest of your life? When you evaluate your present situation, do you still feel challenged and motivated to do your best? Or do you feel stymied from advancing in your career and other areas of your life because you lack the necessary education or expertise? Have you found your true calling, a purpose that inspires and energizes you? Or do you feel uncertain or even ambivalent about what your future holds and the direction you are heading?

Regardless of whether you feel content and satisfied or restless and unhappy with your current life circumstances, it is helpful to periodically step back and reassess your personal and professional trajectory. Where do you see yourself in five years? What unfulfilled dreams do you still hold within you? What steps do you need to take to make them real? The single most important ingredient to a successful life, says Frederic Hudson, is to remain proactive, to continually assess new options, mapping your way into tomorrow with deliberate decisions, risk taking, realism, and caution.

If you really want to jolt yourself into action, imagine the unthinkable—that you are struck by lightning and die. As your loved ones gather at a memorial service to celebrate your life, what will they say? How will they describe your time on this planet, the role you played in their lives, the legacy you left? What immediate changes do you need to make in your life to close the gap between what you would like to be remembered for and what you have achieved toward that end so far.

It has been said that life is a series of single days. To live a full, satisfying life, we must first begin to live full, satisfying days. We strive for the ideal but sometimes don't stop to assess what that ideal means to us personally. Think back to your most recent truly satisfying day when your personal and professional lives really seemed compatible, when everything clicked just right. Now try to pinpoint why that day went so well. Isolate all the particulars, the small incidental things that contributed to that great feeling. Think in terms of seemingly unimportant factors, too, like the weather, how rested you felt, what you ate for breakfast, your pace, and the order of events during the day, if you felt they helped contribute to that contented feeling. Now ask yourself the big question: *What would it take to make that ideal day a real day, day after day?*

> The best way to invent the future you want is to practice imaging it.
>
> *H. B. Gelatt*

Learning for Life

Sooner or later every career gets root-bound. Like a drooping house plant that needs a bigger pot, fresh soil, and a little fertilizer to stimulate growth, so too do our careers. What we wanted at thirty is seldom what we want at forty or fifty. Needs change; priorities change. The measure of a successful life is not what we have achieved at a single point in time, but rather our capacity to continue to grow, to evolve, and to become a more complete person. Each time you "repot" yourself, you focus on new areas of growth and discovery. Maturity is more than a reflection of your chronological age; it is the accumulated wisdom you've drawn from your life experiences.

So who are the role models you have in your circle of friends and colleagues who have reinvented themselves—who have moved out of their comfort zone and taken on new roles, new challenges, and even new careers in an effort to stretch their potential? Pablo Picasso was like that. During the course of his career, he redefined himself several times, changing his style from realism to cubism and experimenting with new media. Laura Ingalls Wilder was in her 50s when she started writing her Little House series. Anna Mary Robertson, better known as Grandma Moses, sold her first painting when she was 78. By the time of her death twenty-three years later, she had painted thousands of pictures and exhibited her work in more than a dozen one-woman shows.

Implicit in these examples is a sense of intentionality, a determination about approaching the future with a well-defined plan. Self-mentoring means taking stock of the parts of yourself you relish and want to preserve as well as those you'd like to change or modify. What is needed is a conscious commitment to move toward personal excellence. Just as we can characterize an organization by its norms of continuous improvement, so too can we characterize individuals by their level of personal commitment to improvement.

Sadly, many people live a life of contingency. They cling to the status quo like a life jacket because they want things to be safe and predictable. They say, "I'll go back to college and get my degree when my kids are in high school" or "I'll look for a new job when things settle down." Others just wait for opportunity to come knocking. But the truth is opportunity doesn't knock. As Bonnie Neugebauer, editor of *Exchange*, says, opportunity is just there, to see or not, to use or pass by. We have to do the hard work. Every day we decide whether to seek out opportunity or to hold steady right where we are. Whether we think there's an opportunity around every corner or that we never get a break is largely up to the way we choose to look at things. If we want our lives to be challenging, dynamic, and energetic, we cannot wait for opportunity to knock. This is wise advice from Bonnie, a woman who has "repotted" herself several times, creating exciting new opportunities in her own life.

Building on Your Strengths

When mapping a journey for career fulfillment, most people figure out what they are good at and what they are not so good at, then they devote their energy to trying to remedy their perceived weaknesses. Marcus Buckingham, author of *Now, Discover Your Strengths*, says this is misguided advice. It is far more important to build on what you do best, on what comes easily—your strengths. He says that in workplaces around the world, people are encouraged to identify, analyze, and correct their weaknesses in order to become strong. He believes this is a flawed assumption. Buckingham advises people to focus on their strengths and find ways to manage their weaknesses. He believes passionately that people excel only by maximizing their strengths, never by fixing their weaknesses.

When people say, "Oh, you are so good at ...," they are usually referring to one of your strengths. A *strength* is something you are able to do consistently well and something from which you derive satisfaction. A strength is a combination of your talents, knowledge, and skill in a specific area. Talents are your naturally recurring patterns of thought, feeling, or behavior—abilities that seem to come naturally. Knowledge consists of both facts and the life lessons you have learned. Skills are the steps, techniques, or actions related to different activities.

So what are your strengths? Are you good at working with people? Are you a whiz at dealing with numbers? Do you have an artistic and creative flair that manifests itself in the way you communicate information? Take a moment to reflect on your strengths as you complete Exercise 10.

exercise 10

What special strengths are you known for, that seem to come easily to you?

_____

_____

In what ways have your major achievements or successes drawn on your strengths?

_____

_____

In what ways does your present position tap your strengths? Do you have an opportunity to do what you do best every day?

_____

_____

Making a Commitment to Action

The future doesn't just happen, it evolves from where we are today—the thoughts we think, the values and beliefs we practice, and the actions we take. If we envision a different scenario for tomorrow, next week, or next year, then we need to create a blueprint for action today.

In completing Exercise 4 in Chapter 3, you've already had a chance to think broadly of the many roles you play, the things that stir your passion, the qualities you want to be known for, the accomplishments you hope to achieve, and the material possessions you hope to acquire during your lifetime. Now let's hone in on your professional identity and think about the knowledge you want to acquire, the skills you want to perfect, and the priorities you want to tackle. Here are some questions to set the stage for the hard work to follow:

- How competent and confident do you feel in your role as an administrator, leader, and advocate for children, staff, and families? In other words, how would you assess your overall knowledge and skill in early childhood program administration in terms of planning, organizing, delegating, computing, writing, budgeting, speaking, listening, motivating, establishing rapport, negotiating, and problem solving?

- How would you assess your personal flexibility? Are you willing to take risks, to think creatively, to move out of your comfort zone, and to approach learning as a lifelong activity?

- How would you assess your relationship with your professional colleagues? Do you feel comfortable in your role as a supervisor? Are you able to interact positively with peers and those in authority? Have you established a network of support to give you candid, honest feedback to guide your professional development?

- How would you assess your overall work attitude and commitment in terms of optimism, self-efficacy, and your willingness to persist in the face of challenges?

Exercise 11 is designed to help you take the next step—to move beyond reflection and self-talk to commit to paper some concrete action steps that will help you strengthen your knowledge and skills, expand your repertoire of positive traits, and broaden your options for the future.

You don't have to see the whole staircase to take the first step.

Martin Luther King Jr.

What are the personal resources you bring to your role as an early childhood administrator—physical, intellectual, social, emotional, and spiritual?

_____

_____

_____

_____

Looking at the competency areas for effective early childhood program administration in Appendix A, select one area that you believe would enhance your effectiveness as a center director and help you meet the challenges you are likely to face during the next three years.

_____

_____

What three action steps could you take to increase your knowledge and skill in this area?

1. _____

2. _____

3. _____

What specific resources in terms of time, money, and support would you need to carry out these action steps?

_____

_____

_____

When you have achieved your goal of improving your performance in this competency area, how will you know it? In other words, what will you be able to do that you can't do now?

_____

_____

_____

We ought to be interested in the future, for that is where we are going to spend the rest of our lives.

Mark Twain

How will you feel when you achieve this higher level of competency?

_____

_____

_____

What percentage of your day do you spend doing things you really like to do? _____%

What percentage of your day do you spend doing things you really dislike doing? _____%

Think of three action steps you could take to increase the portion of your time spent in enjoyable tasks and decrease the amount of time you spend doing things you dislike.

1. _____

2. _____

3. _____

In the list below, circle two new traits or qualities you would like people to use in describing you.

accessible	energetic	humorous	poised
assertive	enthusiastic	innovative	punctual
calm	ethical	inquisitive	reliable
collaborative	fair	inspiring	resilient
compassionate	flexible	introspective	respectful
conscientious	focused	objective	responsible
consistent	friendly	open-minded	resourceful
courageous	generous	optimistic	supportive
creative	good listener	organized	tactful
decisive	gracious	passionate	thoughtful
dependable	helpful	patient	trustworthy
diplomatic	honest	persistent	visionary
empathetic	humble	playful	_____

What specific behaviors do people with these traits or qualities have that might not be part of your current repertoire of behaviors?

_____

_____

_____

What three action steps could you take today that would increase the probability that people would begin using these words to describe you?

1. _____

2. _____

3. _____

Thinking ahead three years, what is one additional priority or goal you'd like to set to ensure that you stay current in professional issues and continue to bring fresh energy and new ideas to your work?

_____

_____

_____

What three action steps could you take during the next six months that would provide evidence that you are serious about achieving this goal?

1. _____

2. _____

3. _____

Remember, your goals must be your own—not goals that someone else has imposed on you. Your action plan should be both *flexible*, allowing room for adjustments as unexpected events occur in your life, and *feasible*, with manageable, doable steps. Plans that are too rigid or too ambitious simply won't get done. If your action plan is well designed, it will be both developmental, providing new skills to improve your ability to be effective in your career, and transformational, providing new experiences and opportunities that broaden your consciousness and self-understanding. Good goals should engender greater feelings of self-efficacy and optimism.

You can't discover new oceans unless you have the courage to lose sight of the shore.

Andre Gide

Japanese corporations have long used the technique of *kaizen,* or small steps for continual improvement, to achieve their business goals and maintain excellence. This simple strategy can help you realize your personal and professional dreams. *Kaizen* recognizes that all changes, even positive ones, are scary. Attempts to reach goals through radical means often fail because they heighten fear. But the small steps of *kaizen* disarm the brain's fear response, stimulating rational thought and creative play.

All *kaizen* asks is that you take small, comfortable steps toward improvement ...

- asking small questions to dispel fear and inspire creativity

- thinking small thoughts to develop new skills and habits

- taking small actions that guarantee success

- solving small problems, even when you're faced with an overwhelming crisis

- bestowing small rewards to yourself or others to produce the best results

- recognizing the small but crucial moments that everyone else ignores

While the steps may be small, what you're reaching for is not. Valuing and maintaining your physical health; embracing the passion, the risks, and the satisfaction of a demanding career; pursuing a rewarding relationship with another human being; or continually revising upward your personal standards, is to strive for powerful goals, often elusive and at times frightening. But for now, all you need to do is make a commitment and take one small step.

From Maurer, R. (2004). *One small step can change your life: The Kaizen way.* New York: Workman.

In his book *Creative Decision Making,* H. B. Gelatt talks about the paradox of goal setting. He recommends that you treat your goals as hypotheses—that you balance achieving them with discovering them. In other words, know what you want, but don't be too sure about it. The bottom line, Gelatt says, is that you should be goal-guided, not goal-governed. Having a clear, precise goal helps focus you on a target so you don't easily become distracted or sidetracked. But concentrating on a clear, precise goal can also be detrimental, because you may overlook other potentially useful options. Gelatt is convinced that wise decision making should be as much a process for discovering goals as it is for achieving them.

In completing Exercise 11, you may well conclude that it's time for you to put up your antennae and begin looking for a new job, one that provides a better fit with your values, aspirations, and capabilities. Or you may decide that it's time to begin sharing your expertise with others through mentoring less experienced directors, writing for publication, giving workshops at professional conferences, or teaching at a community college. Thinking in the future tense also means thinking about leadership succession and how you can put systems in place and begin cultivating in your staff the skills that will sustain quality once you move on to other pursuits.

As you think about your interests and the competency areas you want to strengthen, also think about how you can make yourself unique. What specialized expertise can you cultivate that no one else has? It may be your passion for advocacy about a particular cause or issue, or the way you weave your artistic talents into your administrative role. Your uniqueness can become your passport to success—the expertise that will open doors to new opportunities and bring you personal fulfillment.

Decide and Believe

Decide. If you want to do something, then just decide to do it. If you want to be something, then decide to be it. If you want to have something, then decide to have it. You are what you are, do what you do, and have what you have, all because you decided it. If you had decided something different, then your experience would have been different.

Believe. If you want to be more, do more, and have more, then believe that it's possible. Your belief will manifest itself in your actions and then in your results. The stronger your belief, the faster the results.

From Winget, L. (1996). *The simple way to success.* Tulsa, OK: Win Publications.

Don't Neglect the EI Factor

In thinking about increasing competence, it is easy to focus only on advancing your formal education, bolstering your technical skills, and harnessing your intellectual resources; but success depends on much more than just being smart and analytically adept. The soft skills associated with emotional intelligence are crucial in your work in early care and education. Emotional intelligence includes both abilities associated with personal competence (self-awareness and self-management) and those associated with social competence (social awareness and relationship management).

Emotional intelligence (EI) includes, among other things, your ability to take another person's perspective, to listen empathically, to accurately perceive your own emotions in the moment, to manage your emotional reactions in stressful situations, and to accurately pick up on emotions in other people and understand what is really going on with them. Daniel Goleman, a leading scholar in the EI movement, believes that emotional intelligence defines how we manage behavior, navigate social complexities, and make personal decisions that achieve positive results. He postulates that EI competencies are not innate talents, but rather learned abilities, and that each makes a unique contribution to making people more effective.

Self-Mentoring Strategies

Aldous Huxley once said, "There is only one corner of the universe you can be certain of improving, and that's your own self." Self-mentoring means cultivating your own professional growth through reflection, networking, and seeking out useful resources. The process clearly requires motivation and self-discipline. Here are a few strategies to consider:

- **Observe the behavior of individuals you admire.** Effective leadership is both an art and a science; leadership behaviors can definitely be learned. If there is a person you admire for their listening skills, study the precise behaviors that exemplify good listening. Observe the person's body language and the specific probing questions he or she asks.

- **Talk to individuals you consider to be experts in the field.** Don't be bashful. If there is person you admire for their knowledge in a specific area, contact the individual and ask for advice and resources to build your own expertise in this area.

- **Read, read, read.** Subscribe to journals and magazines that enrich your understanding of different topics of interest. Don't limit yourself to professional journals either. Some of the best wisdom you can get will be from literature in the fiction section of your bookstore. Most important, though, don't just read things that reinforce your point of view. Read articles and books that challenge your assumptions and promote a contrary point of view.

- **Pursue formal coursework.** Consider taking formal courses that will help you attain the degrees, certificates, and certifications that will enhance your vita and open doors to new opportunities.

- **Take risks.** Be bold and audacious and stretch your comfort zone. Challenge yourself to try new things and risk the awkwardness of not being perfect at something.

- **Cultivate a diversified portfolio.** Don't focus on bolstering only your intellect; your emotional, physical, and spiritual sides are just as important. A balanced life has diversity and coherence.

- **Be open to feedback.** Listen fully. Be open to receiving all messages—compliment or criticism—as helpful data in understanding yourself better.

Advocating for Yourself

Donna Shalala, Secretary of Health and Human Services in the Clinton administration and a long-time early childhood supporter, once commented that early childhood advocates often get overlooked in the political process because they are just "too nice." Ouch! It isn't that nice isn't good, it's just that nice sometimes means our needs get ignored, our issues get tabled, and our talents get passed over.

So how do you rate yourself in your ability to advocate for yourself, to speak out about the resources you need and the recognition you deserve? Being serious about mapping your future means having the conviction that what you stand for and represent is worthy of people's time, attention, and support.

Advocating for yourself does not mean you are a self-centered egotist. Nor does it mean you trample on others who get in your way. What it does mean, though, is knowing how to speak so people will listen and knowing how to craft your message so people will care. Advocating for yourself means strategically thinking how you can redefine your roles and your workload to be more fulfilling; to be able to tactfully and sensitively say *no* to requests for your time and talents that do not fit your life plan; and to be able to ask unapologetically for the help and concrete resources you need to move your career forward.

Dilbert reprinted by permission of United Feature Syndicate, Inc.

Developing a Professional Portfolio

Developing and maintaining a professional portfolio is an effective way to document your learning and accomplishments. It can also serve as a powerful tool for career advancement. A portfolio can help you ...

- be clear about your educational and leadership philosophy

- target important goals to work on

- serve as a framework for reflection and self-awareness

- document your professional development activities

- assess and articulate what you have learned

- provide evidence of your knowledge and skills

Think of a professional portfolio as an organizer for learning, a way to document your growth and development as an early childhood professional. It is a way for you to construct your own professional identity. The format or style of your professional portfolio should reflect your unique style and personality. It can be as simple as an accordion file organizer in which you accumulate reflections, artifacts, and certificates or as slick as a leather-bound binder with detailed inserts highlighting your professional journey and accomplishments. If you are a whiz at technology, you can even use a digital format with selected items scanned and organized into an electronic template you've designed.

Some things to consider including in your professional portfolio:

- your current resume

- certificates of attendance from different professional development events

- a copy of your diploma, college degree, CDA credential, teacher certification, or director credential

- a statement of your educational and management philosophy

- examples of presentations you've made (audiotape, videotape, or PowerPoint)

- newsletter, magazine, or journal articles you've authored

- copies of advocacy letters you've written

- photographs documenting important events in the life of your center under your leadership

- a list of professional memberships

- evidence of leadership positions held in professional associations

- examples of work products showing your competence in different areas of early childhood program administration (e.g., a grant proposal you've submitted, your annual budget, a newsletter you've designed, a parent handbook you've written)

- reflections on your professional journey, documenting your growth and learning along the way

Don't think of your professional portfolio only as a collection of work samples you might use to dazzle some future employer, but rather as a vehicle for self-mentoring in which you document your personal insights about your role and the important work you do. When viewed from this perspective, a professional portfolio is both a product and a process—a dynamic, ever-changing reflection of your growth as an early childhood leader.

Soy lo que hago…
Especialmente lo que
Hago para cambiar lo que soy.

> *(I am what I do...*
> *Especially what I do to*
> *change what I am.)*

Edwardo Galeano

CHAPTER 9

A Final Word

Socrates was right! The quest for excellence begins with an inner quest to discover who we are—our passions, values, talents, personal resources, and even those foibles and annoying habits we might prefer not to acknowledge. I hope in reading this book you have experienced the self-affirming insight that comes from identifying the unique gifts you have to offer your organization and the importance of surrounding yourself with others who complement (and not necessarily compliment) your unique skill set and personality.

I also hope the hard work you have done in self-mentoring has strengthened your capacity to rely on yourself as the most important source of information for determining your self-worth. Yes, it is human nature to compare yourself with others, and some comparison is certainly healthy. We all need to know when we are doing well or when we are performing poorly, and it is impossible to make that determination in a vacuum. But living an authentic life means trying to avoid the comparison trap as much as possible.

Consciously avoiding the comparison trap means becoming keenly aware of when and how much you evaluate yourself in relation to others. Comparing ourselves with people we perceive as more capable, more successful, or even better looking (upward social comparison) can provoke feelings of inadequacy, jealousy, frustration, or even hostility. When we compare ourselves with those we perceive as less capable, less successful, or in some way flawed (downward social comparison), we can get a false sense of superiority or entitlement.

In either case, the problem with the comparison game is that it doesn't provide a true reflection of who you really are. It can hijack your self-esteem. The goal of self-mentoring is to be able to look inside and rely on your own internal criteria for measuring self-worth.

Finally, it is my hope that in reading this book you have come to realize that the power of reflection is multiplied when you can turn your own inner dialogue into deep and meaningful conversations with others. Sharing your stories and experiences, talking openly about your hopes and dreams, and taking the risk to engage in frank discussions about values, beliefs, and assumptions is what strengthens human connections.

> You must be the change you wish to see in the world.
>
> *Mahatma Gandhi*

To really understand someone, you need to know what matters most to them in life. What do they value most? How do they define success? What are their beliefs about themselves and about the nature of their chosen work? What is their calling? What do they want out of life? Knowing these things about someone else is a precious gift of friendship. Learning these things about yourself is to step out of your comfort zone, ask some hard questions, make some surprising discoveries, set some new goals, map a new course—to really understand yourself from the inside out.

> *In an average lifetime a person walks about sixty-five thousand miles. That's two and a half times around the world. I wonder where your steps will take you. I wonder how you'll use the rest of the miles you've been given.*
>
> Fred Rogers

For Further Reading

Allen, D. (2003). *Ready for anything*. New York: Penguin Books.

Baldwin, C. (1990). *One to one: Self-understanding through journal writing* (2nd edition). New York: M. Evans and Company.

Baldwin, S. (2002). *The playful adult: 500 ways to lighten your spirit and tickle your soul*. Stillwater, MN: Insights.

Bandura, A. (1997). *Self-efficacy: The exercise of self-control*. New York: Freeman.

Barbe, W., & Swassing, R. (1988). *Teaching through modality strengths: Concepts and practices*. Columbus, OH: Zaner Bloser.

Bateson, M. C. (1989). *Composing a life*. New York: Atlantic Monthly Press.

Baumeister, R. F., & Leary, M. R. (1995). The need to belong: Desire for interpersonal attachment as a fundamental human motivation. *Psychological Bulletin, 117*(3), 497–529.

Bloom, P. J. (2005). *Blueprint for action: Achieving center-based change through staff development* (Revised edition). Lake Forest, IL: New Horizons.

Bloom, P. J. (2003). *Leadership in action: How effective directors get things done*. Lake Forest, IL: New Horizons.

Bloom, P. J. (1999). Images from the field: How directors view their roles, their jobs, and their organizations. In M. Culkin (Ed.), *Managing quality in young children's programs: The leaders role* (pp. 59–77). New York: Teachers College Press.

Bloom, P. J. (1997, November). Navigating the rapids: Directors reflect on their careers and professional development. *Young Children, 52*(7), 32–38.

Bowman, B., (1989). Self-reflection as an element of professionalism. *Teachers College Record, 90*(3), 444–51.

Brooks, D. (April 30, 2001). Time to do everything except think. *Newsweek, 137*(18), 71.

Byrne, R. (2006). *The secret*. New York: Atria Books.

Buckingham, M., & Clifton, D. (2001). *Now, discover your strengths*. New York: The Free Press.

Caffarella, R. S. (1992). *Psychosocial development of women: Linkages to teaching and leadership in adult education*. Washington, DC: Office of Educational Research and Improvement. (ERIC Document Reproduction Services No ED 354 386)

Chodorow, N. (1987). Feminism and difference: Gender, relation, and difference in psychoanalytic perspective. In M. R. Walsh (Ed.). *The psychology of women*. New Haven, CT: Yale University Press.

Carlson, R. (1997). *Don't sweat the small stuff...and it's all small stuff*. New York: Hyperion.

Carter, M. (2006, November/December). Quality enhancement through self-reflecting and dialog. *Exchange,* 14–16.

Crowley, C., & Lodge, H. (2005). *Younger next year for women*. New York: Workman.

Duff, R. E., Brown, M. H., & Van Scoy, I. J. (1995). Reflection and self-evaluation: Keys to professional development. *Young Children*, *50*(4), 81–88.

Duncan, C. W. (2006, July/August). Writing from the heart: Keeping a director's journal. *Exchange*, 70–73.

Dunn, R., & Dunn, K. (1978). *Teaching students through their individual learning styles*. Reston, VA: Reston Publishing.

Ellis, D. (2002). *Falling awake*. Rapid City, SD: Breakthrough Enterprises.

Forrest, R., & McCrea, N. (2002, January). How do I relate and share professionally? *Exchange*, 49–52.

Fromm, E. (1976). *To have and to be?* New York: HarperCollins.

Fulghum, R. (1995). *From beginning to end: The rituals in our lives*. New York: Fawcett Columbine.

Gardner, H. (1993). *Frames of mind: The theory of multiple intelligences* (2nd edition). New York: Basic Books.

Gelatt, H. B. (1991). *Creative decision making*. Menlo Park, CA: Crisp.

Glasser, W. (1976). *Positive addiction*. New York: Harper & Row.

Goleman, D. (2006). Social intelligence: *The new science of human relationships*. New York: Bantam Books.

Goleman, D., Boyatzis, R., & McKee, A. (2002). *Primal leadership: Realizing the power of emotional intelligence*. Boston: MA: Harvard Business School Press.

Green, B. (2006). *The best life diet*. New York: Simon & Schuster.

Gregorc, A. (1982). *An adult's guide to style*. Maynard, MA: Gabriel Systems.

Howell, W. S. (1982). *The empathic communicator.* Belmont, CA: Wadsworth.

Hudson, F. M. (1999). *The adult years.* San Francisco: Jossey-Bass.

Hunt, D. E. (1987). *Beginning with ourselves: In practice, theory, and human affairs.* Cambridge, MA: Brookline Books.

Jensen, B. (2005). *What is your life's work?* New York: HarperCollins.

Jung, C. (1923). *Psychological types.* New York: Harcourt Brace.

Katz, D., Kahn, R., & Adams, J. S. (Eds.). (1980). *The study of organizations.* San Francisco: Jossey-Bass.

Kegan, R. (1994). *In over our heads.* Cambridge, MA: Harvard University Press.

Kelly, G. A. (1955). *The psychology of personal constructs.* New York: Norton.

Kushner, H. (2001). *Living a life that matters.* New York: Knopf.

Lasley, T. (1992). *Promoting teacher reflection.* Journal of Staff Development *13*(1), 24–29.

Maurer, R. (2004). *One small step can change your life: The kaizen way.* New York: Workman.

McGraw, P. (1999). *Life strategies: Doing what works, doing what matters.* New York: Hyperion.

Merrill, D., & Reid, R. (1981). *Personal styles and effective performance.* Radnor, PA: Chilton.

Muller, W. (1999). *Sabbath: Finding rest, renewal, and delight in our busy lives.* New York: Bantam.

Murray, H. (1938). *Explorations in personality.* New York: Oxford University Press.

Myers, I. B. (1998). *Introduction to type* (6th edition). Palo Alto, CA: Consulting Psychologists Press.

Neugebauer, B. (2006, September/October). A manner of speaking. *Exchange,* 95.

Palmer, P. (2000). *Let your life speak: Listening for the voice of vocation.* San Francisco: Jossey-Bass.

Pfeffer, J., & Sutton, R. I. (2000). *The knowing-doing gap.* Boston: Harvard Business School Press.

Rafanello, D. (1996, November). Who do you think you are? *Exchange,* 43–46.

Roizen, M. (2001). *The RealAge (R) workout*. New York: HarperCollins.

Ruiz, D. M. (2001). *The four agreements: A practical guide to personal freedom.* San Rafael, CA: Amber-Allen.

Russo, E. M. (1995). *What's my communication style?* King of Prussia, PA: Organization Design and Development.

Saban, J., Killion, J., & Green, C. (1994, Summer). The centric reflection model: A kaleidoscope for staff developers. *Journal of Staff Development 15*(3), 16–20.

Schön, D. (1987). *Educating the reflective practitioner*. San Francisco: Jossey-Bass.

Schwartz, B. (2004). *The paradox of choice*. New York: HarperCollins.

Seligman, M. (2006). *Learned optimism: How to change your mind and your life*. New York: Random House.

Seligson, M., & Stahl, P. (2003). *Bringing yourself to work*. New York: Teachers College Press.

Selye, H. (1978). *The stress of life* (2nd edition). New York: McGraw-Hill.

Sheehy, G. (1995). *New passages: Mapping your life across time*. New York: Random House.

Shenk, D. (1999). *The end of patience*. Bloomington, IN: Indiana University Press.

St. James, E. (1997). *How to simplify your life*. New York: Hyperion.

Swensen, R. (1998). *Overload syndrome*. Colorado Springs, CO: Navpress.

Vartuli, S. (2005, September). Beliefs: The heart of teaching. *Young Children*, 76–86.

Warren, R. (2002). *The purpose-driven life*. Grand Rapids, MI: Zondervan.

Weil, A. (2006). *Eight weeks to optimum health* (Revised edition). New York: Knopf.

Wheatley, M. (2002). *Turning to one another: Simple conversations to restore hope to the future*. San Francisco: Berrett-Koehler.

Whitmyer, C. (1994). *Mindfulness and meaningful work: Explorations in right livelihood*. Berkeley, CA: Parallax Press.

Winget, L. (1996). *The simple way to success*. Tulsa, OK: Win Publications.

Appendices

A. Program Administration Competencies

B. Communication Style Audit

C. Learning Style Inventory

D. Preferred Perceptual Modality

Program Administration Competencies

Administrators need a strong foundation in the fundamentals of child development, early childhood education, and organizational management in order to guide the instructional practices of teachers and support staff and establish systems for smooth program functioning.

Personal and Professional Self-Awareness

- Knowledge of one's own beliefs, values, and philosophical stance.

- Knowledge of adult and career development, personality typologies, dispositions, and learning styles.

- Ability to evaluate ethical and moral dilemmas based on a professional code of ethics.

- Ability to be a reflective practitioner and apply strategies from a repertoire of techniques to improve the level of personal fulfillment and job satisfaction.

- Knowledge of different professional organizations and resources.

- Ability to reflect on one's personal professional growth and development, set goals for improvement, and take responsibility for one's choices and actions.

Legal and Fiscal Management

- Knowledge of the advantages and disadvantages of different legal structures.

- Knowledge of different codes and regulations as they relate to the delivery of early childhood program services.

- Knowledge of child custody, child abuse and neglect, inclusion, confidentiality, anti-discrimination, risk management, contract, and labor laws pertaining to program management.

- Knowledge of various federal, state, and local revenue sources.

- Knowledge of bookkeeping methods and accounting terminology.

- Skill in budgeting, cash flow management, grant writing, and fundraising.

Bloom, P. J. (2007). *From the Inside Out: The Power of Reflection and Self-Awareness.* Lake Forest, IL: New Horizons. (www.newhorizonsbooks.net)

Staff Management and Human Relations

- Knowledge of group dynamics, communication styles, and techniques for conflict resolution.

- Knowledge of different supervisory styles and career counseling strategies.

- Ability to implement an individualized model of staff development.

- Ability to plan and facilitate group meetings.

- Ability to relate to staff and board members of diverse racial, cultural, and ethnic backgrounds.

- Ability to recruit, orient, and motivate staff to high levels of performance.

- Skill in consensus building, team development, and performance appraisal.

Educational Programming

- Knowledge of different curriculum models, standards for high-quality programming, and child assessment practices.

- Ability to develop and implement a program to meet the needs of young children at different ages and developmental levels (infant/toddler, preschool, school age).

- Ability to implement administrative practices that promote the inclusion of children with special needs.

- Ability to guide teachers in planning and implementing an emerging, bias-sensitive, integrated curriculum that builds on children's abilities and interests.

- Ability to apply child observation and assessment data to planning and structuring developmentally appropriate instructional strategies.

Program Operations and Facilities Management

- Knowledge of state/local regulations and professional standards pertaining to the health and safety of young children.

- Knowledge of nutritional and health requirements for food service.

- Ability to design and plan indoor and outdoor environments that are nurturing, aesthetically pleasing, intellectually stimulating, and psychologically safe.

- Knowledge of playground design, equipment, and safety.

- Ability to implement policies and procedures that help prevent, prepare for, and respond to emergencies.

Family Support

- Knowledge of the diversity of family systems, traditional and nontraditional family structures, parenting styles, and the effect of family dynamics on the development of young children.

- Knowledge of community resources to support family wellness.

- Ability to implement program practices that support families of diverse cultural, ethnic, linguistic, and socio-economic backgrounds.

- Ability to support parents as valued partners in the educational process.

- Ability to demonstrate awareness and appreciation of different cultural and familial practices and customs.

Marketing and Public Relations

- Knowledge of the fundamentals of effective marketing, public relations, and community outreach.

- Ability to evaluate the cost-benefit of different marketing and promotional strategies.

- Ability to communicate the program's philosophy and promote a positive public image to parents, business leaders, public officials, and prospective funders.

- Ability to promote linkages with local schools.

- Ability to develop a business plan and effective promotional literature, handbooks, newsletters, and press releases.

Leadership and Advocacy

- Knowledge of organizational theory and leadership styles as they relate to early childhood work environments.

- Knowledge of the legislative process, social issues, and public policy affecting young children and their families.

- Ability to articulate a vision, clarify and affirm values, and create a culture built on norms of continuous improvement and ethical conduct.

- Knowledge of accreditation standards and ability to evaluate program effectiveness.

- Ability to define organizational problems, gather data to generate alternative solutions, and effectively apply analytical skills in their solution.

- Ability to model healthful lifestyle choices and provide opportunities for staff and children to learn habits that promote health and well-being.

- Ability to advocate on behalf of young children, their families, and the profession.

Oral and Written Communication

- Knowledge of the mechanics of writing, including organization of ideas, grammar, punctuation, and spelling.

- Ability to use written communication to effectively express one's thoughts.

- Knowledge of oral communication techniques, including establishing rapport, preparing the environment, active listening, and voice control.

- Ability to communicate ideas effectively in a formal presentation.

Technology

- Knowledge of basic computer hardware and software applications.

- Ability to use the computer for child care administrative functions.

- Ability to communicate with parents and colleagues via electronic mail.

- Ability to access professional resources on the Internet.

Child Growth and Development

- Knowledge of different theoretical positions in child development.

- Knowledge of the biological, environmental, cultural, and social influences impacting children's growth and development, prenatal through school age.

- Knowledge of the historical roots and philosophical foundations of early childhood.

- Knowledge of developmental milestones in children's physical, cognitive, language, aesthetic, social, and emotional development.

- Knowledge of current research in neuroscience and its application to the field of early care and education.

Communication Style Audit

The following table includes 60 words and phrases organized into 15 rows. Each row includes four descriptors. From each row, select the **one** word or phrase that best captures how you would describe your communication style. When you have finished, you will have 15 circled descriptors, one in each row.

	A	B	C	D
1.	Advocate	Influencing	Steady	Cautious
2.	Decisive	Optimistic	Patient	Restrained
3.	Frank	Enthusiastic	Caring	Exact
4.	Determined	Talkative	Accommodating	Serious
5.	Assertive	Animated	Easygoing	Precise
6.	Achiever	Friendly	Warm	Objective
7.	Take charge	Spontaneous	Counselor	Accurate
8.	Pragmatic	Outgoing	Supportive	Logical
9.	Fast paced	Enjoys the spotlight	Good listener	Orderly
10.	No nonsense	Lively	Sympathetic	Persistent
11.	Honest	Cheerleader	Sensitive	Analytical
12.	Independent	Motivator	Team player	Problem solver
13.	Outspoken	Presenter	Mentor	Organized
14.	Candid	Popular	Sentimental	Detailed
15.	Risk taker	Charismatic	Cooperative	Focused

Bloom, P. J. (2007). *From the Inside Out: The Power of Reflection and Self-Awareness.* Lake Forest, IL: New Horizons. (www.newhorizonsbooks.net)

Scoring of this assessment is straightforward. Simply add up the number of circled words in each column—A, B, C, and D.

- Column A corresponds to a **direct** communication style

- Column B corresponds to a **spirited** communication style

- Column C corresponds to a **considerate** communication style

- Column D corresponds to a **systematic** communication style

The column with the most circled words is your preferred communication style. Some people will have a clear dominant style, while others may be more evenly balanced between two styles or three styles. A description of each style can be found on pages 54–55.

Learning Style Inventory

The following table includes 60 words and phrases organized into 15 rows. Each row includes four descriptors. From each row, select the **one** word or phrase that best captures how you would describe yourself as a learner. When you have completed this part, you will have 15 circled descriptors, one in each row.

	A	B	C	D
1.	realistic	systematic	adaptable	investigative
2.	organized	critical	imaginative	inquisitive
3.	gets to the point	debates	relates	creates
4.	practical	academic	personal	adventurous
5.	precise	analytical	flexible	inventive
6.	orderly	sensible	sharing	independent
7.	perfectionist	logical	cooperative	intuitive
8.	hard-working	intellectual	emotional	risk-taking
9.	product-oriented	quality-oriented	people-oriented	problem-oriented
10.	memorizes	thinks through	collaborates	originates
11.	wants direction	evaluates	spontaneous	changes
12.	cautious	reasons	communicates	discovers
13.	practices	examines	cares	challenges
14.	completes work	gains ideas	sees possibilities	interprets
15.	persistent	rational	aesthetic	experimental

Bloom, P. J. (2007). *From the Inside Out: The Power of Reflection and Self-Awareness.* Lake Forest, IL: New Horizons. (www.newhorizonsbooks.net)

To score this assessment, simply add up the number of circled words in each column—A, B, C, and D. The column with the most circled words is your preferred style, as described below:

- Column A corresponds to a **practical** learning style

- Column B corresponds to an **analytic** learning style

- Column C corresponds to an **imaginative** learning style

- Column D corresponds to an **inventive** learning style

Some people will have a clear dominant style, while others may be more evenly balanced between two or three styles. A description of each style can be found on pages 56–58.

Preferred Perceptual Modality

For each item, indicate the degree to which the statement describes you (0 = *not at all like me*, 1 = *somewhat like me*, 2 = *exactly like me*).

	Not at all like me	Somewhat like me	Exactly like me
1. I can remember the details of what was said at lectures, sermons, and speeches I've attended.	0	1	2
2. I enjoy making things and working with my hands.	0	1	2
3. Even a week after a meeting, I can remember the details of what people wore and where they sat in the meeting room.	0	1	2
4. When attending a workshop, I like to sit up front so I can see the speaker, flip charts, and PowerPoint slides.	0	1	2
5. When attending a workshop, I like to sit near the back of the room so I can get up and move around if necessary.	0	1	2
6. When attending a workshop, I focus on the speaker's tone of voice and how words and phrases are crafted.	0	1	2
7. During workshops, I like to take lots of notes or doodle while I am listening.	0	1	2
8. During workshops and meetings, I rely on handouts, flip charts, and PowerPoint slides to help me process information.	0	1	2
9. I prefer listening to the news on the radio to reading about it in the newspaper.	0	1	2
10. People would describe me as a touchy-feely kind of person.	0	1	2
11. I am skillful at making eye-catching charts and graphs.	0	1	2
12. When someone gives me directions, I don't need to write them down to remember them.	0	1	2
13. When people give me directions, I write down the details so I remember them.	0	1	2
14. I'm good at reading maps.	0	1	2

Bloom, P. J. (2007). *From the Inside Out: The Power of Reflection and Self-Awareness.* Lake Forest, IL: New Horizons. (www.newhorizonsbooks.net)

	Not at all like me	Somewhat like me	Exactly like me
15. I'm good at learning foreign languages.	0	1	2
16. While studying, I tap a pencil, chew on an eraser, fiddle with objects, bite my nails, or run my fingers through my hair.	0	1	2
17. When solving a problem, I weigh options by talking to myself.	0	1	2
18. When I want to recall someone's name, I try to see it pictured in my head.	0	1	2
19. I enjoy listening to books on tape.	0	1	2
20. I would rather read about a new subject than have someone tell me about it.	0	1	2
21. In workshops, I really enjoy interactive exercises and hands-on activities.	0	1	2
22. I'm good at remembering poems, rhymes, and jingles from radio commercials.	0	1	2
23. Some of my best thinking happens when I am running, swimming, walking, or actively moving.	0	1	2
24. I am distracted by visual clutter in a room.	0	1	2
25. I am distracted when participants engage in side conversations while a lecture or presentation is being made.	0	1	2
26. I learn best by doing—actively trying out a new skill.	0	1	2
27. I tend to be neat and detail oriented.	0	1	2
28. I gesture or move around a lot when I speak.	0	1	2
29. I am a good speller. I recognize words by sight.	0	1	2
30. I've always been a whiz at phonics.	0	1	2

To score this assessment, transfer your rating for each item (0, 1, or 2) onto the scoring template below. (Note that the item numbers are not in sequential order). Total the numbers in each column—visual, auditory, and kinesthetic. Scores in each modality—visual, auditory, kinesthetic—will range from 0 to 20. The column with the highest score is your primary perceptual modality. The second highest score indicates your secondary preferred modality. Some people will have a distinct dominance in one of the modalities, while others may be more evenly balanced among two or all three of the modalities. A more complete description of each style can be found on pages 59–60.

Visual	Auditory	Kinesthetic
3. _____	1. _____	2. _____
4. _____	6. _____	5. _____
8. _____	9. _____	7. _____
11. _____	12. _____	10. _____
14. _____	15. _____	13. _____
18. _____	17. _____	16. _____
20. _____	19. _____	21. _____
24. _____	22. _____	23. _____
27. _____	25. _____	26. _____
29. _____	30. _____	28. _____
Total _____	Total _____	Total _____

Available from New Horizons

- Blueprint for Action: Leading Your Team in Continuous Quality Improvement

- Workshop Essentials: Planning and Presenting Dynamic Workshops

- The Program Administration Scale: Measuring Early Childhood Leadership and Management

- The Business Administration Scale for Family Child Care

- Measuring Work Attitudes in the Early Childhood Setting

The Director's Toolbox:
A Management Series for Early Childhood Administrators

- Circle of Influence: Implementing Shared Decision Making and Participative Management

- Making the Most of Meetings: A Practical Guide

- The Right Fit: Recruiting, Selecting, and Orienting Staff

- Leadership in Action: How Effective Directors Get Things Done

- From the Inside Out: The Power of Reflection and Self-Awareness

- A Great Place to Work: Creating a Healthy Organizational Climate

- Inspiring Peak Performance: Competence, Commitment, and Collaboration

A Trainer's Guide is also available for each topic in the Director's Toolbox Series. Each guide provides step-by-step instructions for planning and presenting a dynamic and informative full-day workshop. Included are trainers' notes and presentation tips, instructions for conducting learning activities, reproducible handouts, and a PowerPoint CD.

To place your order or receive additional information
on prices and quantity discounts, contact:

New Horizons Learning Resources, Inc.
616 Smith Ave.
Lake Bluff, IL 60044
Newhorizons4@comcast.net
847.295.8131
www.newhorizonsbooks.net